Teach the Bairns to Cook

soup, vegetables, fish, meat, poultry and game, oatmeal,
puddings and desserts, snacks and savouries

Traditional Scottish Recipes for Beginners

Liz Ashworth

illustrated by children from Lhanbryde
Primary School

Produced in Association with

of Speyside

SCOTTISH CHILDREN'S PRESS

Published in 1996 by

SCOTTISH CHILDREN'S PRESS

Unit 14, Leith Walk Business Centre,
130 Leith Walk, Edinburgh, EH6 5DT
Tel: 0131 555 5950
Fax: 0131 555 5018

In Association with Baxters of Speyside Ltd

SCOTTISH CHILDREN'S PRESS is an imprint of Scottish
Cultural Press

British Library Cataloguing in Publication Data
A catalogue record for this book is available from the British Library

ISBN: 1 899827 23 4

Printed and bound by Cromwell Press, Melksham, Wiltshire

Teach the Bairns to Cook is the first in an
exciting new series of regional recipe books for beginners.
Look out for the companion volume:

Teach the Bairns to Bake
Traditional Scottish Baking for Beginners

1 899827 24 2

Please contact **SCOTTISH CHILDREN'S PRESS**
for further details or for a complete catalogue.

Every man should eat and drink and enjoy the good of all his labour; it is the Gift of God.

Eccl. 3: 13

Contents

Foreword

My family has resided in Fochabers for over 250 years and I am proud that Baxters of Speyside has been helped over the years by a growing band of loyal folk now numbering over 650 – the wider Baxter family. This family enterprise today creates an extensive variety of products made mainly from the superb natural produce of our own Highland area, and they are enjoyed in some 60 countries round the world.

In the 1970s, Liz Ashworth worked in our Product Development Department and, later, she was the able manager of our Staff Canteen. In her 10 years with us before her marriage, Liz proved herself to be an original and creative cook with a gift for expressing her ideas simply yet imaginatively.

Her first book, *Teach the Bairns to Cook*, fills a real need. In my opinion, too little attention is given nowadays to matters of nutrition, diet and teaching our younger folk basic cookery skills. I hope that this book will bring pleasure to children and adults alike, both at school and in the home, and that it will make its own special contribution to keeping our great Scots cookery traditions alive.

Gordon Baxter, President
W. A. Baxter & Sons Ltd
September 1996

Introduction

The aim of this book is to preserve our Scottish traditional recipes and their origins in a simple form. We want to educate and encourage 'the bairns' to make and enjoy these foods so, by kindling their interest, we hope that they, too, will appreciate and keep alive our food heritage.

Each recipe has been graded – simple, intermediate, advanced – and **it is intended that adults will always supervise children** attempting recipes which require cooking or using sharp utensils.

Thanks to my mother for giving me such a love of cooking and for teaching me so well. To Marjory Cairns who sowed the seed of the idea for this book in my mind many years ago. To Mr Gordon Baxter for his enthusiastic support and advice; Mr Gordon kindled my interest in good Scottish food and added to my knowledge and appreciation during my time at Baxters of Speyside.

And thanks to Lhanbryde Primary School, Lhanbryde. To Mrs Allan, the headmistress, and Mrs Robertson, the art teacher, for their help and support. Also to the pupils, who drew all the illustrations. It was very difficult to decide which pictures to include in *Teach the Bairns to Cook* as they were all so exciting and original. Well done. Watch out for more terrific illustrations in the books to follow.

Liz Ashworth
September 1996

Important: Before You Begin to Cook

1) **Always** ask an adult for permission before you cook. If you are unsure or have never cooked on your own before do not be embarrassed to ask for help.

2) Decide on the recipe you would like to make and check how long it will take. Always read the recipe carefully right through before you start. Make sure you understand everything you have to do. Read through the list of ingredients and utensils again and set out everything you will need on the table before you start preparing the dish.

3) Wash your hands really well before you cook or handle food.

4) Always use a chopping board to chop food. Never hold a knife by its blade.

5) Never test hot food with your finger. To taste something, dip in a clean spoon and drop some of the food on to another spoon. Wait until it has cooled before you taste it.

6) Make sure you have a heat-resistant surface to set hot pans and dishes on. A wooden chopping board will do.

7) For safety in the kitchen:

   • Tie back long hair.

   • Wear an apron or overall.

   • Do not wear open shoes or sandals in case of spills.

   • When you are stirring, mixing or beating, put a clean, damp cloth under the bowl to stop it from slipping.

   • Use oven gloves or mitts on both hands to lift hot dishes or pans.

   • Be careful with pots and pans on the hob. Turn the handles inwards so that they can't be knocked off the hob. Be careful that handles do not overhang the hot hob.

   • Always hold the handle of a pan when you are stirring.

8) Remember to turn off the oven, hob, gas or electricity when you have finished using it.

Handy Hints and Measures

Chopping Onions

1 Place the onion on a chopping board and cut off the top and bottom with a sharp knife. Peel off the brown papery skin. Cut the onion in half, from top to bottom.

2 Lay one half of the onion on its flat side. Hold it with one hand and cut it into slices from top to bottom. Then cut across these slices to make small squares. Now do the same with the other half.

Stewing Apples

1 Peel the apples with a potato peeler and use a sharp knife to cut them into quarters. Cut out the stalk and core.

2 Place the apples on a chopping board and cut them into neat, thin slices. Place them in a pan.

3 Add some water – 2 tablespoons of water for every 450g (1lb) apples – and place the pan on a medium heat. Cook for 5 minutes until soft.

4 Taste and add a little sugar until you like the flavour.

Some apples like Brambleys cook very quickly, others cook more slowly – if the apples are still hard after 5 minutes, cook them for a little longer.

Cooking Vegetables

When a recipe asks you to cook vegetables, especially potatoes, try to make sure that they are all of a similar size. Cut them if you need to. If they are different sizes they will cook unevenly and may not be completely cooked in the time stated.

Breaking Eggs

Never break an egg directly into food in case it is bad. Hold the egg over a cup and tap the middle of the shell with a knife to crack it. Carefully, open the shell with your thumbs and let the inside of the egg drop into the cup.

To Measure Half a Teaspoon

Get a knife and smooth the amount on the top of the spoon so that it is flat – this is half a teaspoon and it is sometimes called 'a level teaspoon'.

Pan Sizes

saucepan = a pan which holds 1½–2 pints (1.25 l) of water

stew pan = a pan which holds 3–4 pints (2.5 l) of water

large soup pot = a pan which holds 5–6 pints (3.5 l) of water

Oven Temperatures and Cooking Tips

Your Oven

Check whether your oven is gas or electric. An electric oven can be measured in two ways:

- If your oven shows a temperature range from 0° to 550°, it is measured in degrees Fahrenheit.
- If it shows a range from 0° to 250°, it is measured in degrees Celsius.

Be sure to read the recipe carefully and set your oven to the correct temperature.

Gas Mark			
1	275°F	140°C	low
2	300°F	150°C	
3	325°F	170°C	moderately low
4	350°F	180°F	moderate
5	375°F	190°C	
6	400°F	200°C	moderately hot
7	425°F	220°C	hot
8	450°F	230°C	very hot
9	475°F	240°C	

If You Burn Yourself

- Call for an adult to come and help.
- If your skin is splashed with a hot liquid, or is touched by steam, or you accidentally touch a hot surface, put the affected area under cold running water as quickly as you can. This will take the heat out of the burn. You should keep it in the cold water for about 10 minutes.
- Remember, the quicker you get the burn into cold water the better chance you have of stopping it from blistering and causing permanent scarring.
- You should be very careful around steam and boiling fat or oil. Steam and cooking fat are very hot, hotter than boiling water, and can give you a very nasty burn.

In Case of Fire

- Call an adult.
- Turn off the heat if it is safe to do so.
- Get away from the fire.
- Do NOT put water on it.

Key

Simple Cooking Terms

🎂 **Simple**	Simple, straightforward recipe
🎂🎂 **Inter**	Will require some help
🎂🎂🎂 **Adv**	Will need supervision and help throughout this recipe
1 hr 20 mins	The recipe will take one hour and 20 minutes to make (this time will change for each recipe)
Cook ≋	Needs cooking
No Cook ☒	No cooking required
Hob ◎	Uses the hob
Oven ☐	Uses the oven
Grill ⌘	Uses the grill
E. Wok ○	An electric wok may be used
E. Fry ❖	An electric frying pan may be used
Freeze ❄	Recipe may be frozen

Beat To stir food fast. You can use a spoon, whisk or electric beater.

Boil To cook food over a high heat so that bubbles appear all over the liquid and steam rises from it.

Chop To cut food carefully into small pieces. To chop something FINELY is to cut it up as small as you can.

Dice To cut food carefully into small, equal-sized cubes.

Drain To pour off the liquid which you don't need. You usually use a colander or a sieve which is placed over the sink.

Grate To rub food against a grater so that the food is made into crumbs.

Grease To rub something with butter, margarine or oil. This stops food from sticking to it.

Mash To squash food with a fork or potato masher until it is smooth.

Pinch A pinch is the amount you can hold between your thumb and forefinger (pointing finger).

Simmer To cook food over a very low heat so that it bubbles now and then.

Slice To cut food into thin portions.

Stir To mix ingredients together with a spoon or fork until they are all well blended together.

Soup

Soup has always been one of the main dishes eaten in Scotland as it is filling, nutritious and cheap to make. Folk had to work very hard and they found that soup was easy to make because they could put all the ingredients in the pot and leave the soup to cook while they got on with their other chores.

The name of the pot in which soups or stews were traditionally cooked was 'the kail pot'. It was called this because folk grew a lot of curly kail, a type of cabbage which is easy to grow. Kail was frequently used in soups, broths and stews, and these also came to be called 'kail'.

In time, the name 'kail' was used to refer to the whole meal. An invitation to come and eat a meal would have been:

'Will ye no come and tak yer kail wi me?'

There was a Scottish custom where young girls went out at Hallowe'en to pull a kail 'runt' or stalk. The belief was that a straight, clean stalk meant marriage to a tall, handsome man. On the other hand, a knarled, twisted stalk foretold a match with an ugly, unpleasant, small man!

Cock-a-Leekie

Cock-a-Leekie was very popular in Edinburgh at the time of Sir Walter Scott and Robert Burns. Musselburgh, a nearby town, grew very good leeks and most folk kept poultry in their yards, so they began to cook the two together and made Cock-a-Leekie. Prunes were added to sweeten the soup but a little sugar is just as good.

King James VI of Scotland was very fond of Cock-a-Leekie (sometimes called Cockie-Leekie) and did not like his soup to get cold: 'And, my lords and leiges, let us all to dinner, for the cockie-leekie is a-cooling.' (Scott: *Fortunes of Nigel*)

A much-loved everyday soup, Cock-a-Leekie is also traditionally served at the beginning of a Burns' Supper.

Simple

Serves 4

1 hr 30 mins

Finish the dish with toast

Cook ≋

Hob ◎

E. Wok ○

Freeze ✳

10

HAVE READY

- 75g (3oz) cooked, cold chicken meat
- 1.25l (2 pints) chicken stock – use stock cubes
- 50g (2oz) long-grain rice
- 2 leeks – washed and sliced thinly
- 2 carrots – peeled and finely grated
- pinch ground cloves
- 8 stoned prunes or 1 teaspoon sugar
- 1 tablespoon chopped or dried parsley
- 1 level teaspoon salt
- pinch pepper

- large soup pot
- measuring jug
- potato peeler
- grater
- sharp knife
- chopping board
- wooden spoon
- teaspoon

TO MAKE

1 Chop up the chicken into small pieces.

2 Make up the stock in the pot as it says on the packet. Place the pot on the hob and heat until the stock is boiling.

3 Add the carrots, leeks, rice, cloves.

4 Add the salt and pepper (this is called 'seasoning'), and stir with the wooden spoon.

5 Turn down the heat to low and simmer for 1 hour, stirring occasionally.

6 Add the chicken meat and stir. Cook for a further 15 minutes.

7 Add the parsley and the prunes or sugar.

8 Heat for 2 minutes and then dip in the wooden spoon and drop some of the soup on to a teaspoon. Wait until it has cooled before you taste it. Add some more salt and pepper until you like the flavour.

9 Bring to the boil and serve hot in soup bowls with hot buttered toast.

Cullen Skink

An old Scottish song called 'The Blythesome Bridal' describes a special meal with skink:
'Wi' skink to sup till ye rive [burst], And roasts to roast on a brander
O' flouks [flounders] that were taken alive.'
There is also an old Scots proverb about making skink:
'A spoonfu' o' stink will spoil a patfu' o' skink.' [One bad weed will spoil a plate of soup.]
Cullen Skink is traditional to the Moray Firth. The word 'skink' is Gaelic and means 'essence'.
It was adopted into Scots as another word for soup or a soup-stew (like Cullen Skink).
Making the soup with whole, unboned Finnan Haddock gives a sweeter, richer flavour, but
you can use any smoked haddock.

Have Ready

225g (8oz) whole unboned Finnan Haddock

450g (1lb) potatoes – peeled and sliced

1 medium onion – peeled and chopped

1.14l (2 pints) water

275mls (½ pint) milk

50g (2oz) butter

a little chopped parsley

1 teaspoon salt

3 pinches pepper

large soup pot

large plate

draining spoon

potato masher

knife + fork

To Make

1 Put the fish, onion and potatoes into the pot and cover with the water.

2 Season to taste with salt and pepper.

3 Bring to the boil, then turn down the heat and simmer for 30 minutes until the potatoes are soft.

4 Remove the fish with the draining spoon and place on the large plate.

5 Use the knife and fork to take off the skin and break the flesh into pieces. Remove any bones.

6 Mash the potatoes and onions in the pot.

7 Add the flaked fish, butter and milk.

8 Bring to the boil, stirring all the time.

9 Check the seasoning by tasting the soup, add some chopped parsley and serve.

Simple

Serves 4

1 hr

Cook ≈

Hob ◎

E. Wok ○

11

Tattie Drottle

Potatoes from Ireland were introduced to Scotland in the early 1700s, where they were first grown near Campbeltown. By 1733 they were beginning to be grown in most folk's gardens. This is a creamed potato soup from the North East of Scotland. The best potatoes to use are floury varieties such as Kerrs Pinks or King Edwards. You can freeze Tattie Drottle before the milk is added and then add the milk when you are ready to reheat the soup. Traditionally, Tattie Drottle is served hot with warm oatcakes which are crushed into the soup to make a filling meal.

Simple

Serves 4

1 hr 10 mins

Finish the dish with oatcakes

Cook 〰

Hob ◎

E. Wok ○

Freeze ✳

HAVE READY

850mls (1½ pints) chicken stock – use stock cubes

700g (1.5lbs) potatoes – peeled and sliced

1 small onion – peeled and sliced

25g (1oz) butter

1 celery stalk – finely chopped

275mls (½ pint) creamy milk

pinch of nutmeg

some chopped parsley

level teaspoon salt

2 pinches pepper

large soup pot with lid

sharp knife

chopping board

measuring jug

potato peeler

fork or potato masher

wooden spoon

teaspoon

TO MAKE

1 Put the butter, potatoes and onion into the soup pot. Place on the hob and turn the heat to low.

2 Cook the potatoes and onion gently for 15 minutes. Keep watching them and stir frequently with the wooden spoon. Don't let them brown.

3 Prepare the stock as it says on the packet and pour into the soup pot.

4 Add the celery and sprinkle on the salt and pepper. Put the lid on the pot and simmer for 20 minutes.

5 Remove the pot from the heat and place on a heat-resistant surface. Mash the mixture with the fork or potato masher. You can pass it through a sieve, liquidise or blend it with a hand blender, if you prefer.

6 Add the milk and return the pot to the heat.

7 Add a pinch of nutmeg and some chopped parsley, and mix with the wooden spoon. Taste the soup and add some more salt and pepper until you like the flavour.

8 Serve hot in soup bowls with oatcakes or crusty bread and butter.

Tattie Soup

In 1739 Robert Graham of Tamrawer was very adventurous and planted a field of potatoes near Kilsyth. Many people came from far and near to see this extraordinary novelty and to ask about how the potatoes were grown.

This is a filling, thick soup served by farmers' wives to their menfolk and the farm workers at their midday meal. There are various recipes: this one is from the Highlands and works best if you use floury potatoes like Kerrs Pinks or King Edwards.

HAVE READY

1.75l (3 pints) strong beef or chicken stock – use stock cubes

850g (2lbs) floury potatoes – peeled and sliced

1 large onion – peeled and chopped

half a turnip – peeled and chopped

1 large carrot – peeled and chopped

3 teaspoons salt

3 pinches pepper

large soup pot

sharp knife

chopping board

measuring jug

potato peeler

fork or potato masher

wooden spoon

teaspoon

TO MAKE

1 Prepare the stock cubes as it says on the packet. Make 3 pints of stock in the soup pot.

2 Place the pot on the cooker and heat the stock until it is boiling.

3 Add all the vegetables and the salt and pepper. Mix with the wooden spoon.

4 Simmer for 1 hour until the vegetables are soft.

5 Turn off the heat and set the pot on a heat-resistant surface.

6 Mash all the vegetables with the fork or potato masher until the soup has a rough, porridge-like consistency.

7 Taste the soup and add some more salt and pepper until you like the flavour.

8 Serve Tattie Soup while it is hot. Grated cheese sprinkled on the top melts and tastes terrific!

Simple

Serves 4–6

1 hr 30 mins

Finish the dish with grated cheese

Cook ∿

Hob ◎

E. Wok ○

Freeze ❄

13

Scotch Broth or Barley Broth

In 1786, while he was dining in Aberdeen, Dr Samuel Johnson ate several plates of Scotch Broth and seemed to like the soup. When his friend, Boswell, asked, 'You've never eaten it before?' Johnson replied, 'No sir, but I don't care how soon I eat it again.'
(From Boswell's Journal of a Tour to the Hebrides with Samuel Johnson)

Simple

Needs
overnight
soaking

Serves 8

2 hrs

Cook ≈

Hob ◎

E. Wok ○

Freeze ✳

HAVE READY

- 2.5l (4 pints) strong chicken stock – use stock cubes
- 50g (2oz) pearl barley
- 25g (1oz) dried peas – soaked overnight
- 2 large carrots – peeled and diced
- half a turnip – peeled and diced
- a quarter of a cabbage – finely shredded
- 1 small onion – peeled and diced
- 1 leek – diced
- 3 tablespoons chopped parsley
- 3 teaspoons salt
- 3 pinches pepper

- large soup pot with lid
- bowl
- sharp knife
- chopping board
- measuring jug
- potato peeler
- fork or potato masher
- wooden spoon
- teaspoon

TO MAKE

Put the peas into a bowl, cover with cold water and leave overnight (this is called 'soaking').

1. Peel the carrots, turnip and onion. Cut into small pieces.
2. Wash the cabbage and slice it into thin strips – this is called 'shredding' the cabbage.
3. Wash the leek and the parsley and cut into small pieces.
4. Prepare the stock cubes as it says on the packet.
5. Pour the stock into the large pot and add the barley and all the prepared vegetables. Place the pot on a low heat.
6. Drain the water off the peas which have been soaking overnight and put them into the pot. Add the salt and pepper.
7. Bring to the boil, and reduce the heat until the soup is simmering. Put on the lid. Simmer for 90 minutes.
8. Taste the soup and add more salt salt and pepper until you like the flavour.
9. Add the parsley and serve hot. Once you have tasted Scotch Broth I hope you will want to 'eat it again' too!

You can also serve Scotch Broth as a main meal, eaten with fresh brown bread and butter. For this you will need some extra utensils and ingredients:

HAVE READY

675g (1½lb) boiling beef, mutton or shoulder of lamb

2.5l (4 pints) of water

bowl

plate

2 carving forks

sharp knife

fork

TO MAKE

1 Place the mutton in the large pot and pour in the water. Put the pot on a low heat and simmer for 1 hour.

2 Add the barley, all the prepared vegetables, the drained peas and the salt and pepper to the mutton in the pot. Simmer for 90 minutes.

3 Remove from the heat and set on a heat-resistant surface. Carefully take the meat out of the pot with the carving forks. Put it on the plate and cut into cubes the sharp knife and fork. Trim off any gristle.

4 Add the diced meat to the pot 10 minutes before serving. Turn the heat to medium and make sure that the meat is thoroughly heated through. Taste and add more salt and pepper if you think it needs it.

5 Enjoy your 'soup meal' with fresh brown bread and butter.

The Story of Feather Fowlie

The name Feather Fowlie comes from the French words *oeufs* (eggs) and *files* which means 'dribbled, trickled or spun like threads'.

The Auld Alliance between France and Scotland meant that Scottish cooks adopted many of the French recipes and ways of cooking. James I had a French cook and his successors did, too. In the sixteenth century, the wife of James V, Mary of Lorraine, was French and she introduced French food and customs to Edinburgh. Mary Stuart also liked French food and her love of lavish banquets actually resulted in a food shortage. In 1581 a law was passed in Scotland against 'excessive banqueting'.

An English visitor to Edinburgh in the eighteenth century said:
'At the best houses they dress their victuals after the French manner.'

Hotch Potch

Hotch Potch was obviously a favourite of Sheriff Bell (1803–1874), who wrote:

'Then there's no ilka kindly Scot
Wi mony gude broths he boils his pot,
But rare Hotch Potch beats a the lot,
It smells an smacks sae brawly.'

This soup tastes best when made with fresh garden vegetables, but you can use frozen ones if you wish.

Simple

Serves 8

3 hrs

Cook ≋

Hob ◎

E. Wok ○

Freeze ❋

16

HAVE READY

2.5l (4 pints) strong stock – use stock cubes	large soup pot with lid
4 carrots – peeled	sharp knife
4 small turnips	chopping board
half a small cabbage	measuring jug
1 small lettuce	potato peeler
12 spring onions (syboes)	grater
110g (4oz) garden peas	wooden spoon
110g (4oz) broad beans	teaspoon
2 tablespoons chopped parsley	
2 teaspoons sugar	
3 teaspoons salt	
3 pinches pepper	

TO MAKE

1 Grate two carrots and cut the other two into small pieces.

2 Peel the turnips and cut them into small pieces.

3 Wash the cabbage and cut it into thin strips – this is called 'shredding'. Do the same with the lettuce.

4 Make the stock as it says on the packet. Pour into the pot with all the vegetables (except the grated carrots, half of the peas and most of the parsley). Add the salt and pepper.

5 Place on the heat and bring to the boil, reduce the heat until the soup is simmering. Put on the lid and simmer slowly for 2 hours.

6 Now add the grated carrot, the peas and half of the parsley. Simmer for another 30 minutes.

7 Add the sugar and check the seasoning by tasting the soup. Add some more salt and pepper if you think it needs it.

8 Sprinkle the rest of the parsley on the top and serve – a wonderful, filling soup, thick with summer vegetables.

Vegetables

The traditional vegetables eaten in Scotland are those which can withstand the colder weather and frosts of the Scottish climate. Kail (also known as 'colewort'), is a type of cabbage and was the most popular cultivated vegetable. The crofters grew vegetables in their 'kail yard' – like the vegetable gardens we have today.

Highlanders ate wild plants like nettles, spinach, mustard and wild carrot, which was called 'honey from underground'. Silverweed root was dried and kept in wooden trunks ready for use in the winter, and a plant called 'shemis' was collected from the seashore and eaten as a vegetable, boiled or raw.

Even though potatoes are a very common type of vegetable today, they were not introduced into Scotland until the 1700s, when they were brought over from Ireland. Turnips came from Holland and were first grown by Mr Cockburn of Ormiston in 1725. At this time Scottish gardeners became well known for their knowledge and skill in growing vegetables, and were in great demand abroad. Blair Castle in Perthshire was said to have had one of the best and most beautiful kitchen gardens in the world.

By the 1800s, 'kail wives' (vegetable sellers) appeared in the big towns and cities carrying creels (large baskets which they carried on their backs) full of green vegetables for sale. Artichokes, endive, sea-kale and asparagus, as well as leeks, turnips and cabbage began to be available for everyone to buy.

Kailkenny or Kailkennin

This is from Aberdeenshire, which is in the North East of Scotland. Kailkenny can be eaten on its own, with Skirlie, with a mealie pudding and gravy, or with meat or chicken — which way are you going to eat it today?

Inter

Serves 2

15 mins

Cook ∿

Hob ◎

E. Wok ○

E. Fry ✦

HAVE READY

225g (8oz) cold, cooked potatoes

225g (8oz) cold, cooked cabbage

2 tablespoons cream

½ teaspoon salt

2 pinches pepper

stew pan

wooden spoon

tablespoon

potato masher

TO MAKE

1 Put the cooked potatoes and cabbage into the pan and mash them together with the potato masher.

2 Place the pan on the cooker and turn on the heat to medium. Hold the handle of the pan in one hand and use your other hand to stir well with the wooden spoon.

3 When there is steam coming from the mixture, the food has heated and is hot.

4 Turn the heat to low.

5 Add the cream, salt and pepper, and stir everything together with the wooden spoon. Remember to keep holding the handle of the pan.

6 Heat the mixture for another 5 minutes until the mixture is really hot all the way through.

7 Serve immediately. I bet your whole family will enjoy this special dish.

Colcannon

This dish is traditional to the Highlands. Colcannon is good to eat on its own or with oatcakes and a glass of milk. It is equally good eaten with beef, chicken or game. It is easy to make because you can use any cooked vegetable. I like to make Colcannon with turnips, carrots and cabbage.

HAVE READY

450g (1lb) cold, cooked potatoes

450g (1lb) cold, cooked vegetables, like turnips, carrots, cabbage

50g (2oz) butter

1 dessertspoon brown sauce

½ teaspoon salt

pinch pepper

stew pan

potato masher

wooden spoon

dessertspoon

teaspoon

TO MAKE

1 Put the butter in the pan and place it on the hob. Turn on the heat to low and let the butter melt.

2 Take the pan off the heat and set it on a heat-resistant surface. Add the potatoes and vegetables to the melted butter.

3 Mash everything together with the potato masher. Remove the masher from the pan, tapping it on the side of the pan to loosen any food stuck to it.

4 Put the pan back on the heat and, holding the handle of the pan in one hand, use the wooden spoon to stir the mixture in the pan while it is heating through.

5 Add the brown sauce, salt and pepper. Mix together with the wooden spoon. The mixture should be heated through after 5 minutes. Taste it to check.

6 Remove the pan from the heat and set on a heat-resistant surface.

7 Spoon the Colcannon out on to each person's plate and serve hot.

Inter

Serves 4

15 mins

Cook ∿

Hob ◎

E. Wok ○

E. Fry ❖

Rumbledethumps

'Rumble' meant mashed or mixed together and 'thump' meant bashed down – when you cook this dish you will see how Rumbledethumps got its name. The recipe comes from the Borders and was often eaten as a main meal.

Inter

Serves 2

25 mins

Cook 〰

Hob ◎

Grill ⌘

E. Wok ○

E. Fry ❖

HAVE READY

225g (8oz) cold, cooked potatoes

225g (8oz) cold, cooked cabbage

50g (2oz) grated cheese

25g (1oz) butter

1 small onion – peeled and chopped

small bunch of chives (if you have them)

½ teaspoon salt

pinch pepper

stew pan

2-pint pie dish

plate

saucer

wooden spoon

tablespoon

potato masher

scissors

grater

pair oven gloves

TO MAKE

1 Put the butter in the pan and place on the cooker. Turn on the heat and melt the butter.

2 Add the onion to the melted butter.

3 Hold the handle of the pan in one hand and stir the onion in the pan with the wooden spoon until it is soft but not brown. When you have finished, put the wooden spoon on the saucer (this is called a 'spoon rest').

4 Add the potatoes and cabbage. Use the potato masher to 'rumble' and 'thump' them together.

5 When they are well mixed, tap the potato masher on the side of the pan to remove the food which is sticking to it.

6 Add the salt and pepper. Mix well with the wooden spoon.

7 Turn off the heat and lift the pan off the cooker. Place it on a heat-resistant surface. Hold the chives over the pan and cut into small pieces with the scissors. Stir well.

8 Put the mixture into the pie dish and sprinkle the grated cheese over the top. Turn on the grill to high.

9 Use the oven gloves to place the pie dish under the grill. Keep watching the top to make sure that the cheese does not burn. The cheese will cook in 3 to 4 minutes.

10 When the top of the cheese has turned a nice golden brown, use the oven gloves to take the pie dish out from the grill. Be careful, it will be hot! Set the pie dish on a heat-resistant surface.

11 Spoon the Rumbledethumps on to each person's plate and serve with a glass of milk. This is the kind of snack wee boys and girls ate hundreds of years ago.

Arran Potato Salad

Simple

Serves 4

15 mins

No Cook ☒

Arran potatoes are called 'Arran Chiefs' and are very good in salads because they stay moist and keep their shape and colour when they are cold, but you can use any type of firm potato, like Estima, Maris Bard, Maris Piper or Pentland Squire. There are lots of ways to eat potato salad, see how many you can find. Try it with a barbecue!

HAVE READY

8 cold, cooked potatoes

1 teacup cold, cooked garden peas

a few spring onions (syboes)

1 teaspoon fresh tarragon

1 teaspoon fresh parsley

1 teaspoon fresh chervil

salad bowl

scissors

tea towel

jar with lid

chopping board

wooden spoon

tablespoon

teaspoon

knife + fork

DRESSING

2 tablespoons sunflower oil

1 tablespoon wine vinegar

pinch of sugar

1 teaspoon salt

2 pinches pepper

TO MAKE

1 Place the potatoes on the chopping board and cut them into small squares (about 2cm) using the knife and fork.

2 Put the potatoes into the bowl with the peas.

3 Cut the roots off the spring onions with the scissors and remove any dead outside leaves. Wash the spring onions, tarragon, parsley and chervil well under cold running water and dry them on a clean tea towel.

4 Take the spring onions and hold them over the bowl. Cut them into small pieces with the scissors. Do the same with the herbs.

5 Pour the oil and vinegar into the jar. Add the sugar, salt and pepper. Put the lid on the jar and shake it well for a few minutes to make the 'vinaigrette' dressing.

6 Pour the dressing over the potatoes and herbs in the bowl and then gently stir everything together with the wooden spoon. Try not to break up the potatoes.

7 Arran Potato Salad tastes lovely on a hot summer's day.

Clapshot

Clapshot comes from Orkney and is one of Scotland's best known traditional dishes. It is delicious with oatcakes and it can also be served with Haggis – try it when you make your Burns' Supper on 25 January!

HAVE READY

450g (1lb) cold, cooked potatoes	large soup pot
450g (1lb) cold, cooked turnips	potato masher
50g (2oz) butter	scissors
small bunch chives or spring onions	wooden spoon
½ teaspoon salt	tablespoon
2 pinches pepper	teaspoon

TO MAKE

1 Put the butter into the pot and place it on the hob. Turn on the heat to low and melt the butter.

2 Remove the pot from the heat and set on a heat-resistant surface. Add the potatoes and turnips to the butter.

3 Holding the handle of the pot in one hand and the potato masher in the other, mash the potatoes and turnips together. Remove the masher and tap it on the side of the pot to remove any food which has stuck to it.

4 Clean the chives or spring onions (see opposite page). Hold them over the pot and cut into small pieces with the scissors. Stir in with the wooden spoon.

5 Place the pot back on the heat for 3 minutes, stirring the food with the wooden spoon to make sure it is all heated through. Keep holding the handle as you stir.

6 Add the salt and pepper and stir well. Taste and add more salt and pepper if you think it needs it.

7 Keep heating and stirring the Clapshot until it is steaming hot.

8 Serve with a glass of milk and some oatcakes.

Inter

Serves 4

15 mins

Finish the dish with oatcakes

Cook 〰

Hob ◎

E. Wok ○

E. Fry ❖

Tomato and Syboe Salad

Syboe is the Scottish name for spring onions. This kind of salad is traditionally eaten with brown bread, butter and home-made cheese or with potato salad and cold chicken or game. Salads are nice to make because you can prepare them early and keep them cool in the fridge for a couple of hours until you are ready to eat.

HAVE READY

450g (1lb) firm ripe tomatoes

1 bunch of spring onions (syboes)

DRESSING

2 tablespoons sunflower oil

1 tablespoon wine vinegar

pinch of sugar

1 teaspoon salt

pinch pepper

large flat dish

scissors

fork

sharp knife

chopping board

jar with lid

clean tea towel

tablespoon

teaspoon

TO MAKE

1 Wash the tomatoes under cold running water and dry on a clean tea towel.

2 Cut the roots off the spring onions with the scissors and remove any dead outside leaves. Clean them well under cold running water and dry on a clean tea towel.

3 Pierce one end of a tomato with the fork and use it to hold the tomato on its side. Place it on the chopping board and slice it with the sharp knife. Do this with all the tomatoes.

4 Arrange the tomatoes on the flat dish. Start at the outside and lay one slice overlapping another all round the dish. Then lay another circle of tomatoes and so on until you finish in the middle of the dish – save a nice slice for the middle.

5 Hold the bunch of washed spring onions over the tomatoes and use the kitchen scissors to cut them into small pieces all over the tomatoes.

6 Wash and dry your hands.

7 Pour the oil and vinegar into the jar. Add the sugar, salt and pepper.

8 Screw on the lid tightly and shake for a few minutes to make the salad dressing.

This is a simple vinaigrette dressing. If you like, you can add herbs, mustards, garlic, flavoured oils and vinegars to make different kinds of dressing which will cheer up any salad. Always remember the quantities are 2 times as much oil as vinegar. Pour the oil and vinegar into the jar with all the other bits and pieces you would like, give it a good shake and the dressing is made – easy!

9 Pour the dressing over the tomatoes and spring onions and your Tomato and Syboe Salad is ready to eat.

Neep Purry

Inter

Serves 4

1 hr

Cook ≋

Hob ◎

E. Wok ◗

E. Fry ❖

Freeze ❊

26

'Neep' is the Scottish word for turnip and 'Purry' comes form the French word *puree*, which means 'mashed smooth'.
Sir Walter Scott made up a character called Meg Dods, who was the cook at the Cleikum Inn. In his book, *St Roman's Well*, she recommends adding powdered ginger to Neep Purry. She also says that Neep Purry was best eaten with boiled chicken or veal. Have you any other ideas?

HAVE READY

1 large turnip	large soup pot with lid
25g (1oz) butter	2 sharp knives
¼ teaspoon powdered root ginger	chopping board
boiling water	potato masher
½ teaspoon salt	wooden spoon
2 pinches pepper	colander
	teaspoon

TO MAKE

1 Wash the turnip under cold running water. Peel the turnip and chop it into large, roughly equal sized chunks on the chopping board.

2 Put the turnip into the pot and add 2 teaspoons of salt. Pour enough boiling water into the pan to cover the turnip and then put on the lid.

3 Place the pan on the cooker and turn the heat to high. When the water starts to bubble fiercely and boil, turn down the heat and let it simmer (the water should be just bubbling).

4 Cook the turnip for 40 minutes until it is tender and soft. You can test it with the point of a skewer or knife; it will feel soft all the way through when it is ready.

5 Place the colander into the sink and carefully pour the turnip and water into it to drain the turnip. It's a good idea to run the cold tap at the same time as this will stop the steam blowing up and burning you.

6 Put the turnip back in the pan. Add the butter, ginger, salt and pepper.

7 Holding the handle of the pan in one hand, mash everything together with the potato masher. Take the masher out of the pan and tap it on the side to remove any turnip stuck to it.

8 Put the pan back on the cooker and heat for a few minutes. While it is heating, keep holding the handle and stirring with the wooden spoon.

9 When the turnip is steaming, it is ready to eat.

Fish

Sir Walter Scott in *The Antiquary* said: 'It's nae fish yer buying, it's men's lives'.

The whole family helped to catch fish. The women and children gathered bait by collecting mussels, cockles, lug worms and flounders, and chipping limpets off rocks at low tide. Women also helped the men to bait the fishing lines.

Fishing was done in boats called 'yawls'. Each yawl usually held three men who rowed or sailed out to sea depending on the wind. They kept their food – usually oatcakes and cheese, with water to drink – in a canvas bag called a 'poken mor'. The women carried the fishermen out to the yawls on their backs because the leather sea boots which the men wore were not fit for wading through the salty seawater! The fish they caught was dried, smoked or sold fresh by the fisherwife who carried it round the countryside in a basket called a 'creel'. She either sold the fish or bartered it in exchange for other food, such as fruit and vegetables.

There is a famous song written by Lady Nairne (1766–1845) called 'Caller Herrin'. 'Caller' means fresh and this used to be the common cry of fisher folk as they stood selling their fish:

Buy m' caller herrin
They're bonnie fish and halesome farin?
Buy m' caller herrin
New drawn frae the Forth.

Caller herrin! Caller herrin!

Wha'll buy m' caller herrin?
They're no brought here wi'out brave darin
Wives and mithers maist despairin
Ca them lives o men.

Caller herrin! Caller herrin!

Finnan Haddie

Finnan or Findon Haddocks are named after a small village six miles south of Aberdeen.
Some folk like Finnan Haddie topped with a poached egg.

Inter

Serves 1

20 mins

Finish the dish
with toast or a
poached egg

Cook

Hob ◎

E. Wok ○

E. Fry ❖

30

HAVE READY

1 skinned fillet of smoked haddock	stew pan with lid
1 egg	saucepan
25g (1oz) butter	plate
1 teaspoon cornflour	sieve
1 teacup of milk	sharp knife
1 teaspoon vinegar	teacup
salt + pepper	draining spoon
	wooden spoon
	teaspoon

TO MAKE

1 Cut the fish into four pieces. Melt the butter in the stew pan, add the fish and sprinkle it with a little pepper.

2 Put the pan on a high heat and let the butter bubble. Turn down the heat, put on the lid and simmer for 5 minutes.

3 Mix the cornflour with a little of the milk in the teacup. Stir in the rest of the milk.

4 Pour this over the fish and shake the pan gently to cover the fish with the mixture. Keep the heat low and cook for 5 minutes until the milk thickens and makes a sauce.

5 While it is cooking, poach the egg:
   (a) Put 4 cups of water into a small saucepan. Add a pinch of salt and the vinegar. Bring to the boil.
   (b) Break the egg into the cup. Reduce the heat until the water is just bubbling and carefully pour in the egg.
   (c) After 3 to 4 minutes the egg will have set. Remove it from the pan with the draining spoon.

6 Remove the fish from the pan with the draining spoon and place it on the plate.

7 Stir the sauce quickly to remove all the lumps. If there still lumps, pour the sauce through the sieve on to the fish.

8 Top with the poached egg and serve with hot buttered toast.

Ham an Haddie

This recipe comes from the Moray Firth. It is traditional to fry Ham an Haddie but grilling is healthier and the fish keeps all its juices and flavours. Fish was grilled on a metal bar called a 'brander' which lay across the top of an open fire.

In the North East of Scotland the phrase 'ham an haddie' means slap dash, or untidy.

HAVE READY

2 fillets of smoked haddock – skinned	grill pan
225g (8oz) bacon rashers	saucepan
	2 plates
25g (1oz) butter	teacup
2 eggs	draining spoon
50mls (2 tablespoons) double cream	fish slice
1 teaspoon vinegar	tongs
salt + pepper	oven gloves

TO MAKE

1 Heat the grill to a medium temperature.

2 Grease the bottom of the grill pan with some of the butter. Lay the fish fillets on the butter. Put small pieces of butter all over the fish and sprinkle with a little salt and pepper.

3 Lay the rashers of bacon on the fish. Use the oven gloves to place the grill pan under the grill. Cook for 5 minutes.

4 While they are cooking, put on the eggs to poach:

  (a) Put 4 cups of water into the saucepan. Add a pinch of salt and the vinegar. Bring to the boil. Reduce the heat until the water is just bubbling.

  (b) Break one egg into the cup and carefully pour it into the water. Do the same with the other egg.

  (c) After 3 to 4 minutes the eggs will have set. Use the draining spoon to take them from the pan.

5 After 5 minutes, remove the grill pan from the heat with the oven gloves and set on a heat-resistant surface.

6 Pour the cream over the bacon and fish.

7 Turn the grill to high. Cook the cream-covered bacon and fish until the cream starts bubbling – takes 2 to 3 minutes.

8 Place the fish, bacon and some of the cream sauce on to warm plates and top with a poached egg.

Inter

Serves 2

20 mins

Finish the dish with a poached egg

Cook

Grill ⌘

Arbroath Smokies

Originally these were made by the fisherwives in a village in Angus called Auchmithie and so they were first known as Auchmithies. They were also known as Closefish, Pinwiddies or Luckens. Arbroath Smokies, as they are now called, are made with fresh haddocks which have been cleaned and gutted but not split open. They are tied together in pairs by the tails and hung on wooden spits over fires made of wood chips. This cooking process is called 'hot smoking'. Smoking gives the fish a special taste and makes it keep for a longer time than fresh fish.

Simple

Serves 1

25 mins

Finish the dish with brown bread and butter

Cook 〰

Oven □

E. Wok ○

E. Fry ❖

32

HAVE READY

one Arbroath Smokie per person

a little butter

salt + pepper

aluminium foil

baking tray

large plate

fish slice

draining spoon

knife + fork

oven gloves

TO MAKE

1 Heat the oven to Gas 4, 350°F or 180°C. Alternatively, boil 275ml (half a pint) of water in a wok or electric frying pan.

2 Open the the fish and spread the butter over the inside. Sprinkle with a little salt and pepper and close the fish.

3 Cut a piece of foil large enough to wrap up the fish.

4 Place the fish on the foil and wrap the foil around it.

5 Lay the parcel of fish on a baking tray and, using oven gloves, lift it into the oven. (If you are using a wok or an electric frying pan, place the fish into the hot water, put on the lid and turn the heat low.) Cook for 15 minutes.

6 Use oven gloves to take the baking tray from the oven. Set it on a heat-resistant surface. (If you are using a wok or frying pan, lift the fish on to the plate with a draining spoon.)

7 Leave the parcel to cool for 3 minutes, then carefully open it. Watch out for the steam which will escape.

8 Use the fish slice to lift the fish on to a plate and remove the bones and skin with a knife and fork.

9 Serve the juicy, smoky fish with fresh brown bread and butter.

Tatties an Herrin

Herring are at their best before they spawn (lay their eggs). Some herring spawn in the spring but the herring on the west coast of Scotland spawn in the autumn: so every summer the fishermen used to go to the west coast to catch herring before they spawned. The unmarried women followed the herring fleet to gut, salt and pack the fish into barrels. This is a traditional Scottish fisherman's meal. It was cooked in a large pot hung on a hook (called a 'swee') over the open peat fire.

HAVE READY

4 herring fillets

450g (1 lb) potatoes – peeled

water

1 dessert spoon salt

large soup pot with tight-fitting lid

potato peeler

sharp knife

chopping board

fish slice

colander

draining spoon

heat-proof plate

TO MAKE

1 Cut the potatoes into equal-sized pieces and put them into the pot. Cover with fresh cold water and add the salt. Place on the heat and bring to the boil.

2 Put on the lid, reduce the heat slightly and boil for 15 minutes.

3 Take the pot off the heat and pour off most of the water.

4 Carefully, place the herring over the potatoes in the pan using the fish slice. Put on the lid, turn down the heat to low and return the pot to the cooker.

5 Cook the herring and the potatoes. Small herrings will be cooked in 10 minutes, larger herring will take 15 minutes.

6 Lift the herring out on to the plate with the draining spoon. Shake a little salt over the herring and keep them warm.

7 Place the colander in the sink. Empty the potatoes into it to drain off the rest of the water. Put the potatoes back in the pot and place on the heat. Shake them until they are dry.

8 Serve the hot potatoes with the fish. As well as being really tasty, herring are very good for you.

Inter

Serves 4

1 hr

Cook ≋

Hob ◉

E. Wok ○

E. Fry ❖

33

Salt Herrings

The herrings which were not eaten fresh were put in wooden barrels with lots and lots of salt. The salt preserved the fish and meant folk had food during the winter months when fresh fish was scarce. Today salted herrings can be bought from the fishmonger.
Salt herrings were traditionally eaten with potatoes because the potatoes took away the saltiness. In some parts of the country the salt herrings are cooked in the same pot as the potatoes, exactly the same way as for Tatties an Herrin. You can do the same: follow the recipe for Tatties an Herrin, but use salt herrings instead (remember to soak them overnight in cold water before using) and don't add any extra salt during cooking.

Inter

Needs overnight soaking

Serves 1

15 mins

Finish the dish with potatoes

Cook 〰

Hob ◉

E. Wok ○

E. Fry ❖

HAVE READY

one salt herring per person

saucepan with tight-fitting lid

deep dish

plate

draining spoon

TO MAKE

Lay the herring in a deep dish, cover with cold water and leave overnight. This is called 'soaking'.

1 Lift the fish out of the water and put it into the pan. Cover the fish with fresh, cold water and put the pan on to the cooker.

2 Turn on the heat and bring to the boil, then reduce the heat until the fish is just moving in the water.

3 Cook for 10 minutes.

4 Remove the fish from the pan using the draining spoon, and lay it on to a plate.

5 Serve the herring with boiled potatoes and butter. Delicious!

Soused Herring

Herring was one of the main fish caught in Scotland and so people invented many different ways to eat it. This recipe serves the fish cold. 'Soused' herring means that the fish has been steeped or cooked in a special mixture called a 'marinade'.

HAVE READY

4 herring fillets	casserole dish with lid
2 bay leaves	2 plates
8 peppercorns	draining spoon
1 teacup of water	oven gloves
1 teacup of vinegar	
salt	

TO MAKE

1 Put on the oven to heat at Gas 2, 300°F, 150°C.

2 Lay the herring on a plate, skin side down. Shake some salt over it.

3 Take the tail of the fish in your fingers and roll it up until you reach the head. The skin should be on the outside. Place the rolled-up fish in the casserole dish.

4 Lay the bay leaves and peppercorns on top of the fish. Pour the water and vinegar over the fish and put on the lid.

5 Use the oven gloves to put the casserole into the oven. Cook for 1 hour.

6 Take the fish out of the oven with the oven gloves. Place on a heat-resistant surface and leave to cool for about 2 hours.

7 When it is cool, use the draining spoon to lift the fish on to the plate.

8 Serve the fish with a nice crispy salad of lettuce, tomatoes, cucumber, carrots and apple, and crusty brown bread.

Simple

Needs left to cool for 2 hrs

Serves 4

1 hr 10 mins

Finish the dish with mixed salad and brown bread

Cook ∿

Oven ☐

35

Hairy Tatties

So that the fisher families would have food when fresh fish was scarce, they salted and dried fish by hanging them from the rafters in the roof of the kitchen. It was common to preserve cod and ling in this way. As the fish hung it became very hard indeed.
This is the way to cook dried fish.

Inter

Needs overnight soaking

Serves 2

1 hr 20 mins

Finish the dish with oatcakes

Cook 〰

Hob ◎

E. Wok ○

E. Fry ✦

36

HAVE READY

175g (6oz) dried fish

450g (1lb) potatoes – peeled and cut into equal-sized pieces

150mls milk

2 teaspoons salt

2 saucepans with tight-fitting lids

large plate

potato peeler

sharp knife

draining spoon

wooden spoon

potato masher

TO MAKE

Put the dried fish into a dish, cover with cold water and leave overnight (this is called 'soaking').

1 Use draining spoon to remove the soaked fish from the dish. Put it into a pan and cover with fresh cold water. (Throw away the water in the dish.)

2 Turn on the heat and bring to the boil. When the fish is bubbling, turn down the heat until the fish is just moving in the water in the pan. Cook for 1 hour.

3 Cook the potatoes while you are waiting. Put them into a pan with the salt. Cover with cold water and place on the hob. (If you are using a wok or electric frying pan, cook the fish first, remove it with a draining spoon and set it aside before cleaning the pan. Then cook the potatoes.)

4 Turn on the heat and bring the potatoes to the boil. Then turn the heat down until the water is just bubbling.

5 Cover with a lid and cook for 20 minutes.

6 Test the potatoes by pushing the tip of a knife into one – if it feels soft all the way through, the potatoes are ready. Carefully drain off the water – watch out for the steam!

7 Mash the potatoes with the potato masher and then pour in the milk. Mash the potatoes and milk together until they are smooth (no lumps!).

8 When the fish has cooked for 1 hour, turn off the heat. Lift the fish on to a plate with the draining spoon.

9 Put the fish into the pan with the potatoes and mix them together with a wooden spoon.

10 Serve with crisp oatcakes and a glass of milk – do you know why they are called Hairy Tatties? Maybe you can guess when you eat them!

Baked Kippers

Kippers are herrings which have been gutted, split down the middle from head to tail and lightly salted. Then they are put on to racks in a smoking shed where they are left to hang for 8 hours in a smoky atmosphere. This process is called 'cold smoking'. It means that the fish is not heated and is therefore not cooked while it is being smoked. Smoking the fish gives it a special flavour and makes it keep longer than fresh fish.

It is said that the best kippers come from Loch Fyne on the west coast of Scotland.
Kippers can be baked, fried, grilled or boiled.

Simple

Serves 1

20 mins

Finish the dish with brown bread and butter

Cook 〰

Oven □

HAVE READY

one kipper per person

10g (½oz) butter

pyrex baking dish with lid

large plate

fish slice

knife + fork

oven gloves

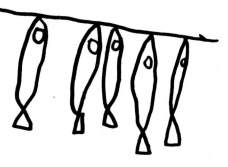

TO MAKE

1 Arrange the shelves in the oven so that the dish will sit on the middle shelf. Heat the oven to Gas 4, 350°F or 180°C.

2 Lay the kipper skin side down in the dish and put some small pieces of butter all over it.

3 Put the lid on the dish.

4 Use oven gloves to put it on to the middle shelf of the oven. Bake for 15 minutes.

5 Carefully remove the dish from the oven and take off the lid with the oven gloves.

6 Use the fish slice to lift the kipper on to the plate.

7 Remove the bigger bones with the knife and fork.

8 Serve the hot buttery kipper with some nice fresh brown bread and butter.

Boiled Kippers

Boiled Kippers are delicious! You can eat them on their own, with a knob of butter on top, or with some hot crusty bread.

HAVE READY

2 kippers

25g (1oz) butter

stew pan with lid

large plate

fish slice

knife + fork

TO MAKE

1 Place the kippers in the pan and cover with cold water.

2 Put the pan on the hob and turn on the heat.

3 Bring to the boil and when the water starts to bubble turn off the heat.

4 Leave the fish in the hot water for 5 minutes.

5 Remove the pan from the heat and set on a heat-resistant surface.

6 Lift the kippers out of the water with the fish slice – watch, they will be hot – and place each kipper on the plate, skin side down.

7 Use the knife and fork to remove the larger bones. Put half the butter on top of each kipper and watch it melt to a lovely golden pool. Now take a mouthful – it tastes wonderful!

Simple

Serves 2

10 mins

Finish the dish with hot crusty bread

Cook 〰

Hob ◎

E. Wok ○

E. Fry ❖

Cabbie Claw

Cabbie Claw comes from the French word *cabillaud* which means 'cod'. Cod is the main ingredient in this dish.

Inter

Serves 4

I hr

Finish the dish with mashed potatoes

Cook ∭

Hob ◎

E. Wok ○

E. Fry ❖

40

HAVE READY

900g (2lbs) cod fillet	stew pan with lid
I pkt white sauce mix	2 saucepans
2 eggs	2 small bowls
275ml (½ pint) milk	pyrex casserole dish
sprig of parsley	plate
small piece of horseradish or teaspoon horseradish sauce	teacup
	wooden spoon
kettle of boiling water	draining spoon
I teaspoon salt	teaspoon
pinch pepper	knife + fork

TO MAKE

1 Hard-boil the eggs:
   (a) Place the eggs in the saucepan and cover them with cold water.
   (b) Put on the heat and bring to the boil.
   (c) Boil for 10 minutes.
   (d) Turn off the heat and lift the eggs out of the pan with the draining spoon. Place in a bowl of cold water.

2 While the eggs are cooking, put the fish into the stew pan. Add the parsley, horseradish, salt and pepper.

3 Carefully pour enough boiling water over the fish to just cover it. Put the pan on the heat and watch as the water begins to boil.

4 Turn down the heat and simmer the fish very gently for 20 minutes.

5 When the eggs are ready and while the fish is cooking, make the sauce:
   (a) Pour the sauce mix into the small bowl.
   (b) Use the teaspoon to stir in a little of the milk to make a creamy mixture. Make sure there are no lumps.

6 Put the rest of the milk into the saucepan, place it on the cooker and turn on the heat.

7 When the milk is beginning to steam, remove the pan from the cooker and very carefully pour the hot milk into the bowl. Stir it well and then carefully pour it all back into the pan.

8 Put the pan back on to a low heat. Hold the handle with one hand as you stir the sauce in the pan with the wooden spoon until it becomes thick and begins to bubble. Turn the heat down very, very low.

9 Remove the shell from the hard-boiled eggs by tapping the shells on a hard surface. You can then peel off the shells. Rinse the eggs in cold water to remove any bits of shell which are still sticking to them.

10 Chop the eggs on a plate with the knife and fork. Add them to the sauce and mix well.

11 By this time the fish will be ready. Turn off the heat and lift the fish out of the water with the draining spoon. Put it into the casserole dish.

12 Cut the fish into small chunks using the knife and fork. Pour the sauce over the fish and it is ready to eat.

13 Serve the fish with creamy mashed potatoes, and enjoy this wonderful meal.

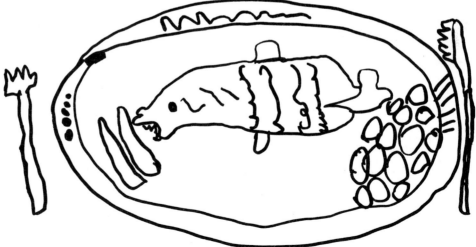

Tweed Kettle

In the eighteenth century the food shops in Edinburgh sold a popular dish called Tweed Kettle, commonly known as 'Salmon Hash'. The salmon was cooked, added to a sauce and eaten with mashed potatoes.

If you make some mashed potatoes you can eat the hot salmon and potatoes together just as they did in Edinburgh nearly two hundred years ago. Sometimes they mixed in mushrooms which had been cooked in butter, or some chopped, hard-boiled egg. Perhaps you would like to try this?

Inter

Serves 4

1 hr

Finish the dish with mashed potatoes

Cook ♒

Hob ◎

E. Wok ○

E. Fry ❖

HAVE READY

450g (1lb) fresh salmon fillets with skin removed

1 fish stock cube

2 spring onions (syboes) or small bunch of chives

½ pint boiling water

1 tablespoon chopped parsley

1 teaspoon salt

pinch pepper

stew pan with lid

large plate

heat-proof measuring jug

fish slice

ladle

scissors

sharp knife

wooden spoon

tablespoon

teaspoon

TO MAKE

1 Put the fish stock cube in the measuring jug and pour in the boiling water. Stir with wooden spoon until it has dissolved.

2 Lay the salmon fillets on the large plate and cut into pieces (about 5cm or 2 inches) with the sharp knife. Put the salmon into the stew pan. Wash and dry the large plate.

3 Sprinkle the salt and pepper over the salmon.

4 Wash the spring onions (syboes) or the chives under cold running water. Remove any dead outside leaves and trim off the tops of the leaves with the scissors. Hold the onions or chives over the fish and snip them into small pieces using the scissors.

5 Pour in the stock and put the pan on the hob. Turn on the heat and watch until the liquid begins to bubble.

6 Turn down the heat to low and put the lid on the pan. Cook for 30 minutes.

7   Turn off the heat and take the lid off the pan – watch out for the steam which will escape. Sprinkle the parsley on top of the fish.

8   Carefully use the draining spoon to take the salmon out of the pan and place it on the large plate.

9   Use the ladle to pour the juices over the fish.

10 Serve immediately with mashed potatoes – imagine you are in the eighteenth century and enjoy your Salmon Hash!

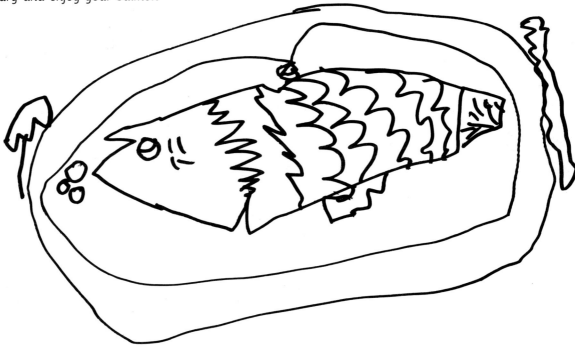

A Salmon Slice

Inter

Serves 1

20 mins

Finish the dish with peas and new potatoes

Cook ≈

Hob ◎

E. Wok ○

E. Fry ❖

Freeze ❋

44

At one time salmon was so plentiful in Scotland that it was given to people who worked on estates and farms as part of their payment for the work they did. They were given so much salmon that they grew tired of it, and went on strike, refusing to go back to work until they were promised more variety in the food they were given!

Sir Walter Scott writes that the best way to eat fresh salmon is to have a huge pot of salted water boiling on a fire at the riverside. The freshly caught salmon was cleaned, gutted, cooked in this large pot and eaten the moment it was ready.

This recipe is just as delicious. Remember: eat your salmon as soon as it's cooked!

HAVE READY

110g (4oz) salmon steak

10g (½oz) butter

salt + pepper

stew pan with lid

aluminium foil

scissors

knife

plate

draining spoon

TO MAKE

1 Cut a large square of aluminium foil big enough to wrap around the fish.

2 Lay the fish in the middle and sprinkle with salt and pepper.

3 Cut the butter into pieces and place small pieces of butter all over the fish. Wrap up the fish in the aluminium foil.

4 Put about 20cm depth of water into the pan and put the fish into the cold water.

5 Place the pan on the heat and bring the water to the boil.

6 Boil for 2 minutes. Turn off the heat. Leave the parcel of fish in the pan for 5 minutes.

7 Lift out the fish with the draining spoon. Lay it on the plate.

8 Unwrap the fish very carefully (watch out for the steam).

9 Now, get your knife and fork working and enjoy the lovely taste of buttery salmon, new tatties and baby peas – I don't think you will want to go on strike like the workers did long ago!

Meat

People who lived in the towns and cities during the eighteenth century spent much of their free time in places called 'taverns'. This was because there were very few public entertainments – they didn't have television, cinemas, swimming-pools or ice rinks! Most of the ordinary folks' houses were so small that there was hardly any room for them to sit, relax and enjoy their evening meal, so they went to the taverns. The women who ran many of the taverns were called 'Luckies' (meaning 'mistress of the household'). Each tavern was well known for its own special dishes: Lucky Wood's tavern in the Canongate in Edinburgh, for example, was famous for mutton hams, roast leg of lamb and goose pie. Allan Ramsay (1685–1758), one of Scotland's greatest poets, was a customer and wrote that she dished up 'gude belly-baum' – plenty of good food to eat.

At that time the bells of St Giles in Edinburgh not only rang on Sundays to call folk to church, but also rang on weekdays. Like the way your school bell tells you when it is playtime or lunch time, the St Giles' bell rang at 11.30 a.m. for 'Meridian' (elevenses), at 2 p.m. for dinner (this bell was called the Kail Bell) and at 8 p.m. to tell people that the day's work was over. This bell was called the 'Tinkle-sweetie'.

Minced Collops and Mashed Tatties

The word 'collop' comes from the French word escallop, which means 'a small piece of meat'. Minced Collops and Mashed Tatties is one of the best known of all the Scottish dishes. In days gone by it was even eaten at breakfast time!

Inter

Serves 4

45 mins

Finish the dish with mashed potatoes

Cook ∭

Hob ◎

E. Wok ○

E. Fry ❖

Freeze ❋

HAVE READY

350g (12oz) steak mince

1 heaped tablespoon pinhead oatmeal

1 large onion

450g (1lb) potatoes

25g (1oz) butter

150ml (1 gill) milk

275ml (about ½ pint) boiling water

2 teaspoons salt

2 pinches pepper

stew pan with lid

saucepan with lid

sharp knife

chopping board

small bowl

colander

potato peeler

potato masher

wooden spoon

tablespoon

dessertspoon

teaspoon

TO MAKE

1 Place the onion on the chopping board and cut it into small pieces (see page 6). Using the flat blade of the knife, scrape the onion into the small bowl.

2 Put the mince into the saucepan and put the pan on to the cooker. Turn on the heat to high and keep stirring as the mince starts to cook. Break up any lumps with the wooden spoon. Soon it will start to sizzle and turn brown.

3 When it is all browned, lower the heat and add the onion, oatmeal, 1 teaspoon of salt and the pepper. Stir well with the wooden spoon.

4 Carefully pour the boiling water into the pan. Stir with the wooden spoon, then turn the heat very low until the mince is just bubbling.

5 Put on the lid and leave to cook for 30 minutes. Check it every 10 minutes – take off the lid (watch out for the steam!) and stir with the wooden spoon to make sure that the meat does not stick to the bottom of the pan. Add more water if you think it is becoming too thick.

A handy tip is to put a saucer on the worktop beside the cooker. This is called a 'spoon rest' and will hold the wooden spoon when you are not using it. You can buy specially made spoon rests in the shops (a present for Mum perhaps?).

6 While the mince is cooking, you can peel the potatoes with the potato peeler.

7 Cut the potatoes to the same size, put them into the stew pan with a teaspoon of salt and cover them with cold water. Put the pan on to the cooker and turn the heat on high.

8 When the potatoes are boiling, turn down the heat until they are bubbling and then put on the lid. The potatoes will take 20 minutes to cook. Test them after 20 minutes by pushing the tip of a sharp knife into one; if the inside feels soft the potatoes are ready.

9 Turn off the heat. Place the colander in the sink and empty the potatoes and water into it to drain off the water. Run the cold tap at the same time, this stops the steam from rushing up and scalding you.

10 Put the potatoes back in the pan and add the butter.

11 Place the pan on a heat resistant surface and make sure that it is steady. Hold the handle of the pan in one hand and mash the potatoes with the potato masher to break them up.

12 Pour in the milk and keep mashing until they are smooth. Tap the masher on the side of the pan to remove the potato. Put the lid on the pan to keep the potatoes hot.

13 By this time the mince will be ready. Turn off the heat, remove the lid and give the mince a stir.

14 Taste the mince and add some more salt and pepper until you like the flavour. Adding a little salt, pepper, spices or herbs to meat, fish, poultry and vegetables helps to make them taste even better – this is called 'seasoning'.

15 Serve the Minced Collops and Mashed Tatties on to each person's plate. Enjoy your meal – I wonder if you are having them for breakfast!

Skirlie (Skirl-in-the-pan)

Skirl means a very loud noise, like the 'skirl of the pipes'. This dish is called Skirlie because it makes a loud sizzling noise when it is being cooked in the pan. To make Skirlie in the traditional way means using very hot fat, so here is a recipe which is easier and safer to make. It also uses less fat so it is better for you too!

Skirlie was traditionally served with meat (especially Minced Collops), poultry, game, even cod and mustard sauce! Often it was eaten as a quick meal with mashed potatoes and a glass of milk — for quickness, you can make some instant mashed potatoes to eat with your Skirlie. Try Skirlie and potatoes for a snack — it is really good and is more exciting than a sandwich!

HAVE READY

110g (4oz) medium oatmeal

1 small onion – peeled and chopped

½ pint chicken or vegetable stock – use a stock cube

12g (½oz) fat from cooked meat or margarine (cooking oil will do)

25g (1oz) chopped suet

1 teaspoon salt

stew pan with lid

chopping board

sharp knife

wooden spoon

tablespoon

teaspoon

TO MAKE

1 Chop the onion (see page 6). Put it in the pan with the fat. oil or margarine, and suet. Place the pan on the hob.

2 Cook for about 5 minutes on a low to medium heat, until the onions are soft and golden. Keep stirring with the wooden spoon while they cook.

3 Pour the stock into the pan slowly and very carefully.

4 Turn down the heat a little and then add the oatmeal, stirring all the time with the wooden spoon. If the oatmeal is dry and crumbly, add a little more water until it becomes soft.

5 Add the salt and stir well.

6 Turn down the heat to very low and cook for 5 minutes, stirring to prevent the oatmeal sticking.

7 Turn off the heat and put the lid on the pan.

8 The Skirlie is now ready to eat. You can serve it on its own or leave it in the pan and reheat it when the rest of the meal is ready.

Snap and Rattle

Snap and Rattle is the name given to a plate of Minced Collops and Mashed Tatties served with hot sizzling Skirlie. It was called this because of the snapping, rattling noise made as the hot Skirlie was dished on to the mince. Why don't you try it? Simply cook both of the recipes above and serve them together – Snap and Rattle tastes really good!

Scots Pies or Tuppenny Pies

These small pies were one of the first kinds of 'Fast Food' in Scotland. They usually cost two pennies and so were called Tuppenny Pies. They are made of a pastry (called hot water pastry) which is strong and crisp. This is made into little round boxes and filled with spicy minced meat before the lid is popped on. Traditionally, people used mutton for the filling. When the pie was cooked the rim above the lid was often filled with hot gravy, potatoes, peas or beans to make a meal.

Butchers and bakers still sell Scots Pies in Scotland today, but now they cost a bit more than two pence!

Belmont Pie

This recipe was given to me by a cook called Doris Low who used to work 'in service'. Working 'in service' meant that you had to live at the place where you worked. Holidays were very short, perhaps only a few days each year, and you were only allowed half a day off each week. The day's work was long and hard, and in return you were given a uniform to wear, food to eat, a place to sleep and a small amount of money as wages. The money was only paid out once or twice a year.

Inter

Serves 4

1 hr 10 mins

Finish the dish with fresh vegetables

Cook ∿

Oven ☐

Freeze ✳

HAVE READY

350g (12oz) cold, cooked mince

BATTER TOPPING

110g (4oz) flour

25g (1oz) margarine

1 egg

275ml (½ pint) milk

1 heaped teaspoon baking powder

½ teaspoon salt

2-pint pie dish

mixing bowl

balloon whisk

sieve

small plate

knife

teacup

wooden spoon

tablespoon

teaspoon

oven gloves

TO MAKE

1 Arrange the shelves in the oven so that the pie dish can sit on the middle shelf with room for the pie to rise. Switch on the oven at Gas 5, 375°F or 190°C.

2 Put the mince into the bottom of the pie dish and smooth flat with the back of the tablespoon. Wash the spoon.

3 Now to make the batter topping. Put the sieve on top of the mixing bowl. Pour the flour into the sieve and then use the back of the tablespoon to push the flour through into the bowl. This is called 'sieving' and the reason we do this is to put air into the flour which makes whatever we are baking lighter and nicer to eat.

4 Add the salt and baking powder and mix in.

5 Put the margarine on to the plate and cut it into small cubes with the knife.

6 Add the margarine to the flour in the bowl.

7   Wash and dry your hands really well and roll up your sleeves. Put both your hands in the bowl of flour with the palms facing up. Practice rubbing your thumb along all your fingers from your little finger to your index (pointing) finger. Now, using your hands, mix and rub the flour and margarine together by rubbing them with your thumb and fingers as you have practiced. Keep on doing this until all the lumps of margarine have disappeared and the mixture in the bowl looks crumbly.

8   Wash the flour and margarine off your hands.

9   Using the balloon whisk, make a hollow in the centre of the crumbly mixture.

10   Break the egg into the teacup and then pour it into the hollow. Add half the milk and stir all the ingredients together with the wooden spoon.

11   Gradually pour in the rest of the milk while you beat it together with the whisk.

12   Pour over the mince in the pie dish. Use the oven gloves to put the dish into the oven. Be careful not to burn yourself.

13   Bake for 45 minutes until the top has risen and turned golden brown all over. Take the dish from the oven: remember to use oven gloves!

14   Serve with some fresh green vegetables, like buttery spring cabbage or runner beans.

If you are going to freeze Belmont Pie make sure you take a note of the date it was made and eat it within 8 weeks.

You can make all sorts of different pies using left-over meat or chicken and gravy. You can even put fish and sauce under the batter. Have you any other ideas?

Sea Pie

No one really knows how Sea Pie got its name but I think it was probably made and eaten by sailors and fishermen when they were at sea. Sea Pie can be made with stewed meat or mince.

Inter

Serves 4

40 mins

Finish the dish with vegetables

Cook ≋

Hob ◎

E. Wok ○

E. Fry ❖

Freeze ❋

HAVE READY

450g (1lb) cold, cooked mince or stew

PASTRY TOPPING

175g (6oz) self-raising flour

75g (3oz) ready-prepared suet

150ml (1 gill) water

1 teaspoon baking powder

½ teaspoon salt

stew pan with lid

mixing bowl

rolling pin

sieve

2 wooden spoons

tablespoon

teaspoon

oven gloves

TO MAKE

1 Put the cooked mince or stew into the stew pan with a cup of water and put on the cooker. Turn the heat on at low to heat the meat through.

2 Place the sieve over the bowl and pour in the flour and baking powder. Use the back of the tablespoon to push the flour and baking powder through the sieve into the bowl.

3 Put the sieve to one side and add the suet and salt.

4 Pour in the cold water and mix with the wooden spoon until all the ingredients make one soft, sticky ball in the bowl. (Add more water if it feels too stiff.) This is called a 'dough'. Dough is also the name given to bread before it has been cooked.

5 Wash and dry the worktop and wash your hands.

6 Shake some flour over the worktop and tip the dough out of the bowl on to the flour. Sprinkle more flour on top. The flour is used to stop the dough sticking to your hands and the worktop.

7 Rub some flour on the rolling pin and then use it to roll the dough flat. Try to roll it into the shape of the stew pan.

8 Wash and dry your hands.

9 The meat in the pan should now be hot. Stir it with a wooden spoon to make sure that it has not stuck to the bottom of the pan. You need plenty of gravy in with the meat because the pastry will soak up the liquid as it is cooking, so add some more water if there is not much gravy and stir well.

10 Turn up the heat and let the meat boil for a minute.

11 Turn down the heat until the meat is just bubbling and carefully place the pastry on top of the meat in the pan. Put the lid on the pan and make sure the heat is still at a low setting. Leave the pie to cook for 20 minutes — until the pastry has risen and looks like a scone.

12 The pie can also be cooked in a casserole in the oven at Gas 4, 350°F or 180°C. If you decide to cook it this way, leave the lid off the casserole dish to give a crisper pastry.

13 Serve the Sea Pie with buttered carrots and broccoli. While you are eating your Sea Pie imagine you are on board a ship in the 'mess room' (the dining-room of a ship) with the crew. The salty air is said to give us a good appetite so tuck in!

If you are going to freeze Sea Pie, make sure you take a note of the date it was made and eat the pie within 8 weeks.

Stovies

The name 'Stovies' comes from the French word *etouffe*, which means cooked in a closed casserole or pot. Stovies are 'stoved' which means they are cooked in a closed pot on the hob of the cooker. Some old recipes describe the cooking as being 'stoved until done'.

There are many, many recipes for Stovies. Some add only onions, others add turnips and carrots, meat, chicken and, on the island of Colonsay in the Hebrides, they added limpets to the Stovies as they were cooking!

Inter

Serves 4

1 hr 45 mins

Finish the dish
with oatcakes

Cook

Hob ◎

E. Wok ○

E. Fry ❖

HAVE READY

225g (8oz) left-over stew, mince or roast

675g (1½lb) potatoes – peeled

2 large onions – peeled and chopped

50g (2oz) good beef dripping – you can buy this at the butcher's

2 teaspoons salt

pinch pepper

stew pan with lid

sharp knife

chopping board

wooden spoon

teaspoon

TO MAKE

1. Place one of the peeled potatoes on the chopping board. Use the sharp knife to cut the potato in half. Put the flat side on the board and, holding the potato in one hand, cut the potato into slices. Do this with the rest of the potatoes.

2. Put the dripping into the pan and put it on the cooker. Turn on the heat to low and melt the dripping.

3. When the fat has melted, add the onions and increase the heat to medium.

4. Stir with the wooden spoon until all the onions are browned. Turn down the heat to very low.

5. Put the sliced potatoes into the pan.

6. Add the salt and pepper. Stir with the wooden spoon.

7. Cover the pan with the lid and cook over a very low heat for about 30 minutes until the potatoes are soft and breaking. Remember to stir every 15 minutes to make sure that nothing sticks to the pan.

A kitchen minute timer is useful for this: set the timer to beep every 15 minutes to remind you to stir the pan. It's also a good idea to have a saucer to put your spoon on – this is called a 'spoon rest'.

8 Add the left-over stew, mince or roast meat (cut the roast meat into small pieces on a plate first, using a knife and fork). Stir it into the mixture in the pan and heat through for about 30 minutes on a low heat. Stir occasionally to stop it sticking.

9 Taste the mixture and add some more salt and pepper if you think it needs it. Stir well. Taste again until you like the flavour.

10 Serve in mounds on heated plates with an oatcake stuck in the top. Pour out a glass of ice cold milk to drink with your Stovies and enjoy a traditional Scottish meal. Poorer families ate their Stovies without any meat at all and drank buttermilk (the milk left over when butter is made) with them.

Forfar Bridies

Forfar is a farming community on the east coast of Scotland in the county of Angus and it is famous for these delicious meat pasties. Originally, Maggie Bridie, who came from nearby Glamis, made these pies and sold them at the local fairs and cattle markets, and that is how they got their name.

Inter

Serves 4

1 hr 15 mins

Cook ≋

Oven □

Freeze ❊

HAVE READY

450g (1 lb) rump steak, topside or salmon cut of beef

2 medium onions – peeled and finely chopped

450g (1 lb) ready-made shortcrust pastry

75g (3oz) ready-prepared suet

flour to roll out pastry

1 teaspoon salt

2 pinches pepper

rolling pin

baking tray

sharp knife

chopping board

mixing bowl

tablespoon

teaspoon

large plate (about 15cm or 6″ across)

pastry brush

teacup

oven gloves

TO MAKE

1 Arrange the shelves in the oven so the baking tray can sit on the middle shelf. Heat the oven to Gas 6, 400°F or 200°C.

2 Place the meat on the chopping board and use the sharp knife to trim off the fat and gristle. Cut into pieces roughly 2cm in size.

3 Put the meat, suet, onions, salt and pepper in the bowl and mix well with the tablespoon.

4 Clear away the chopping board. Wash the worktop and dry it with a clean tea towel ready to roll the pastry.

5 Wash and dry your hands really well.

6 Shake some flour over the worktop and dust the rolling pin with flour. This is to stop the pastry from sticking. Put the pastry on the flour and roll it out until you can fit four circles the size of the plate into it.

7 Lay the plate face down on the pastry and cut round it with the sharp knife. Do this four times.

8 Divide the meat mixture equally between the circles of pastry, covering one half with the meat and leaving 0.5cm round the edge.

9 Put some cold water in the teacup and use the pastry brush to wet all round the edges of the pastry.

10 Fold the pastry over the meat to make a half-circle shape. Press down the edges with your finger tips to make sure that they are sealed.

11 Make a small hole in the top with the point of the knife. This hole lets the steam escape while the meat is cooking and stops the pastry from becoming soggy.

12 Rub a little cooking oil over the baking tray with a piece of kitchen towel. Place the bridies on the tray and use the oven gloves to put them in the oven. Bake for 20 minutes.

13 Turn down the oven heat to Gas 4, 350°F or 180°C and bake for another 35 minutes.

14 Use the oven gloves to take them from the oven and set them on a heat-resistant surface. Let them cool a little and then eat them the way the farmers did – Forfar Bridies were eaten by folk as they sat or stood around chatting at the markets and fairs. They are ideal snack and picnic food and make a delicious change from sandwiches!

Bacon Floddies

These are a savoury potato cake made in parts of the country where they kept pigs and so had plenty of bacon. It is traditional to serve Bacon Floddies with pickled beetroot, but you can also try them with a salad, crusty bread and butter or even baked beans.

Adv

Serves 2–3

30 mins

Cook ∭

Hob ◎

E. Wok ◑

E. Fry ❖

HAVE READY

I large potato – peeled and grated

I small onion – peeled and finely chopped

50g (2oz) bacon – finely chopped

25g (1oz) white cap mushrooms

I egg

vegetable oil for frying

pinch of thyme (if available)

½ teaspoon salt

pinch pepper

frying pan

mixing bowl

baking tray

sieve

sharp knife

chopping board

cup

fork

potato peeler

kitchen towel

grater

tablespoon

teaspoon

TO MAKE

1 Peel the potato. Wash it in cold water and dry it on some kitchen towel.

2 Place the grater in the mixing bowl and then grate the potato by holding the grater with one hand and rubbing the potato up and down the grater with your other hand until all the potato is grated.

3 Chop the onion into small pieces (see page 6 if you have never done this before). Put it into the bowl with the potato.

4 Put the mushrooms into the sieve and hold them under cold running water to wash them. Dry them on kitchen towel or a clean tea towel and put them on the chopping board.

5 Cut one of the mushrooms in half through the stalk. Lay the flat side on the chopping board. Hold the mushroom steady and use the sharp knife to cut it into strips. Then cut across the strips to make small squares. Do this with all the mushrooms and then put the chopped mushroom into the bowl with the potato and onion. Wash and dry the knife and chopping board.

6 Lay the bacon flat on the chopping board. Cut it into strips with the sharp knife, then cut across the strips to make small squares. Add the bacon to the bowl.

7 Add the salt, pepper and the thyme to the bowl.

8 Break the egg into the teacup and, holding the handle, beat it with the fork to mix the white and yolk together, then pour this into the bowl. Stir it all together with the tablespoon.

9 Pour enough oil into the frying pan to cover the bottom and put it on the heat. Heat the frying pan until the oil sizzles when a piece of bread is dropped into it (this is a handy way to test cooking oil or fat to make sure that it is the correct temperature).

10 Drop tablespoonfuls of the mixture into the fat. Be careful to stand back so that the hot fat does not splash and burn you. Cook over a low to medium heat, turning once so that both sides are golden brown.

11 Drain on the baking tray covered with kitchen towel and serve hot. What will you choose to eat with your Floddies?

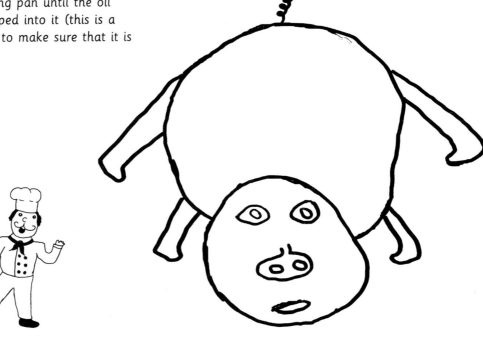

Haggis

Inter

Serves 6–8

3 hrs

Cook ♒

Hob ◉

E. Wok ○

60

Haggis is the traditional Scottish dish that we all eat on Burns' Night – 25 January – which was his birthday. Robert Burns's friend, Andrew Bruce, who was a merchant in Edinburgh, invited him to a family meal at his home and it was here that Burns first tasted Haggis. He enjoyed eating it so much that he wrote a special poem called 'Ode to a Haggis'. This poem is now recited over a hot Haggis as part of the celebrations during a Burns' Supper – called 'Addressing the Haggis'. When the speaker comes to the verse which describes how good the inside of the Haggis is, he plunges a dagger into the Haggis. Everyone cheers, whisky is drunk as a toast and the Haggis eaten with Chappit Tatties (mashed potatoes) and Bashed Neeps (mashed turnips).

The name 'Haggis' comes from the French word *hachis* which means to chop. Although Haggis is thought of as a Scottish dish, it is also found in the Mediterranean countries. It is known to have been eaten in Roman times during the reign of Emperor Augustus, and an ancient Greek writer called Aristophanes mentions a type of Haggis in his book, *The Clouds*. The original recipe for Haggis uses a mixture of liver, lites and heart mixed with oatmeal and seasoning which was stuffed into the stomach bag of a sheep. This recipe is a simple version avoiding the sheep's stomach!

HAVE READY

450g (1lb) minced ox heart

450g (1lb) minced ox liver

225g (8oz) minced steak

1 onion – chopped

110g (4oz) chopped suet

110g (4oz) pinhead oatmeal

2 teaspoons salt

1/4 teaspoon pepper

large soup pot with lid

mixing bowl

aluminium foil

thick rubber band

tablespoon

pudding bowl

oven gloves

TO MAKE

1 Put all the minced meats into the mixing bowl. Add the suet, onion, oatmeal, salt and pepper. Mix well with the tablespoon.

2 Place the pudding bowl upside down on the aluminium foil and cut a piece that is twice the size of the top of the bowl. Make sure that there is a little extra all the way round which can be turned over the rim. Fold the foil in two.

3 Put the pudding bowl into the pot and pour in enough water to come one third up the outside of the bowl. The bowl is going to sit in this water in the pot. Take the bowl out, put the lid on the pot, and set it on the cooker. Turn the heat on full so that the water will come to the boil.

4 Put the meat mixture into the pudding bowl and cover it with the doubled piece of aluminium foil. Put the rubber band around the rim to hold the foil on to the bowl.

5 When the water is boiling, carefully remove the lid – watch out for the steam! – and lower the pudding bowl into the water in the pan using oven gloves.

6 Lower the heat until the water is just moving in the pan and replace the lid. Cook for 2 hours 30 minutes. This is called 'steaming'. Check the pan every 30 minutes to make sure that the water has not boiled dry.

7 After the cooking time is over, turn off the heat and very carefully take the pudding bowl out of the pan – use oven gloves! Carefully remove the foil lid, keeping the opening away from your face because steam will escape from under the foil.

8 Your haggis is ready to eat!

If you wish, you can make your own Burns' Supper using the recipes in this book!

Menu

Cock-a-Leekie Soup

-·-·-·-·-·-·-·-·-·-·-

Haggis with Clapshot

-·-·-·-·-·-·-·-·-·-·-

Flummery

Get a copy of 'Ode to a Haggis' so you can address your own haggis! Play a tape of bagpipe music in the background. Enjoy your Burns' Supper!

Potted Hough

This traditional method of cooking meat meant that the cheapest joint – called 'Hough' – could be made into a tender and tasty dish. This is especially good with mashed potatoes, brown sauce and salad.

Inter

Needs left overnight

Serves 6–8

5 hrs

Cook ≈

Hob ◎

62

HAVE READY

one knap bone (from the butcher)

2lb hough of beef (also called shin)

3.5l (6 pints) cold water

3 teaspoons salt

large soup pot with lid

several bowls or plastic containers, like margarine tubs

large plate

draining spoon

ladle

sharp knife

fork

teaspoon

TO MAKE

1 Put the hough on to the plate and cut off all the fat with the sharp knife. (The meat appears to be quite gristly, but do not cut this away.) Cut the meat into large pieces and then put it into the pot. Throw the fat away.

2 Wash and dry the plate and knife.

3 Wash the bone under cold running water and put it into the pot with the meat.

4 Add the salt and cover the meat and bone with the cold water.

5 Lift the pot on to the hob and turn the heat to medium. When the water is boiling, turn down the heat until the water is bubbling slowly. Put the lid on the pot and leave to cook for 4 hours.

6 Turn off the heat and leave to cool a little.

7 Use the draining spoon to lift the meat out of the pan and place it on the plate.

8 Use the knife and fork to cut the meat into small pieces. Remove any gristle or fat left after cooking.

9 Half fill each bowl or plastic container with meat.

10 Use the ladle to take enough cooking liquid out of the pan to cover the meat in the containers. (If there is any liquid left in the pan, keep it – it is ideal for making soup.)

11 Stir gently with the fork and then leave overnight in a cool place.

12 In the morning you will find that the mixture has set and you have a delicious meat jelly. It makes a tasty sandwich filling for your lunch box!

The Story of Sheep's Heid

At one time Sheep's Heid was a very popular meal and was eaten by both rich and poor people. The oldest public house in Scotland (dating from the 1500s) is in the village of Duddingston, near Edinburgh, and is called 'The Sheep's Heid'. Travellers used to rest here if they were making a long journey and enjoy a meal of Sheep's Heid, for which the inn became famous. Customers included Mary Queen of Scots, Bonnie Prince Charlie and King James VI of Scotland who presented the inn with a decorated, mounted ram's head.
To make the dish the sheep's heid was 'singed' (the skin and hair were burnt off) and then it was soaked overnight in cold water. The following day it was covered in fresh cold water. Vegetables, barley and seasoning were added and it was all boiled for a long time – as much as eight hours! The cooking liquid was served as soup, then the meat from the heid was eaten with a sauce which was made from some of the broth thickened with flour and butter.
Fleshers (as butchers were called) used to give a gift of a sheep's heid to their best customers on a Saturday. Dr Cullen (a famous doctor) felt that Sheep's Heid broth was good for you and he even prescribed it for his patients.

The Story of Mutton Ham

In the days before refrigeration was invented to keep food fresh, various ways were used to preserve food for the winter. Sheep farmers cured and smoked legs of mutton in the same way as pig keepers cured and smoked pork to make ham, and so the cured mutton was called 'Mutton Ham'. Mutton Ham became a Scottish speciality, and in the eighteenth century the Scottish borders were famous for the Mutton Hams which they produced. Mutton Hams were even exported from Glasgow to the West Indies and America!

The only time crofters in the Highlands ate fresh meat was when the sheep were killed to be cured as Mutton Ham for the wintertime; then they were able to eat some of the meat fresh before it was salted and smoked. The meat was soaked in a brine (salty water), herb and spice mixture for 10 to 14 days which pickled and preserved the meat. Then it was removed from the brine and soaked for four hours in fresh water before being dried. The Mutton Ham was hung over a peat or hardwood fire which had juniper berries or a juniper branch in the embers and was left in the smoky atmosphere for 10 to 14 days.

To cook Mutton Hams they were covered with cold water and boiled for 30 minutes per pound of meat. The meat could be eaten hot or cold and was often served for breakfast.

Poultry and Game

POULTRY

For centuries people paid each other with goods instead of money. This is called 'bartering'. Even in the cities, people kept chickens in their back yard. The chickens provided eggs and could be killed for food, but they were also used to pay debts. As a result of this custom, there was hardly any need for actual money so there was not much of it around.

After 1603 (the Union of the Crowns of Scotland and England) when the nobles of the Scottish Parliament had to travel to London to sit in the Houses of Parliament, they found that their small amount of money did not go very far and they were not so well off as they had been in Scotland. They used to say 'Bang goes sixpence!' because their money disappeared so quickly.

Even as late as 1773 Samuel Johnson found that in St Kilda (a Hebridean island off the west coast of Scotland) 'money was not yet known!'

GAME

The game birds found in Scotland are grouse, capercaillie, blackcock, ptarmigan, partridge, wild duck, pheasant, woodcock, snipe and quail. At one time they were all shot and used for food; however, nowadays some of these birds are very rare and are protected. Game birds are counted in twos called 'brace', so a brace of grouse means two grouse. The birds feed mostly on heather and this gives the flesh a special taste.

White grouse or ptarmigan live on the very high slopes of the mountains and have also been found in the Arctic. The birds turn white in the wintertime so that their enemies will not see them in the snow – this is called 'camouflage'.

Black grouse or blackcock are smaller than the capercaillie but larger than the red grouse. They are easily spotted because they have glossy blue-black feathers.

Red grouse live mostly on the moorlands of Scotland and North England. They are thought to be the best-tasting game birds and are shot from 12 August until 10 December. On 12 August – known as 'The Glorious Twelfth' – the first grouse to be shot are rushed to the airports and flown to the restaurants in the south of England – they are considered to be a great delicacy.

Capercaillie is the largest member of the grouse family. They live in hilly pine forests and can be very fierce. The male looks like a turkey when his tail is fanned in display. They nest in the undergrowth beneath the trees or on open high ground and they eat pine needles, which gives the flesh a strong smell and taste. As a result, the birds have to be cleaned as soon as they are shot. People used to stuff an onion into the body cavity and then bury the bird for up to five days. This was supposed to take away the strong piney taste. If it did not work they buried the capercaillie and forgot about it altogether!

The capercaillie is now very rare.

Pheasants live mostly on lower ground, where they eat grain and plants. As a result, they are larger than grouse and their flesh does not have such a strong flavour. Pheasants are at their best from November to January.

Rabbits were a popular meat for most folk as they were the easiest for people to catch!

The most common breed of deer to be found in Scotland is Red Deer. The stags (males) are at their best in early autumn after summer feeding. Hinds (females) are shot from October to February. Hind meat has less fat than stag meat and so has less flavour. The Highlands of Scotland now have many farms which breed deer for their meat, which is called venison. It is healthy meat to eat because it is low in fat.

Howtowdie

This recipe comes from the Edinburgh area and uses a large pan to 'pot roast' a chicken. The name is from the French word *le hutaudeau* which means a young chicken.
Nettle Kail is another version of Howtowdie which was made in the Highlands and Inner Hebrides. The crofters ate nettles in the springtime when they were tender. They thought the nettles would purify their blood after the long winter, so they added them to the kail pot along with the cooking fowl.

Adv

Serves 6

3 hrs

Finish the dish with vegetables

Cook ∿

Hob ◎

E. Wok ○

E. Fry ❖

Freeze ✳

68

HAVE READY

1kg 35g (3lb) roasting chicken

25g (1oz) butter

12 shallots (or small bunch of spring onions)

a little grated nutmeg

few sprigs of fresh thyme (if available)

teacup of hot water

FOR THE STUFFING

110g (4oz) medium oatmeal

1 medium onion

50g (2oz) suet

1 teaspoon salt

pinch pepper

large soup pot (big enough to hold the chicken) with lid

sharp knife

mixing bowl

2 plates – 1 large and 1 small

2 skewers

carving knife

2 carving forks

spoon

draining spoon

clean tea towel

teaspoon

TO MAKE

1 Chop the onion into small pieces and put them in the bowl (see page 6 if you have not done this before).

2 Add the oatmeal, suet, salt and pepper. Mix well together. That's the stuffing made.

3 Wash the inside of the chicken – hold it under a cold tap and let the water run through it and over it. Dry it with a clean tea towel and lay it on the large plate.

4 Peel the shallots, put them on the small plate and leave them to one side.

5 Find the skin flap which is at the neck of the chicken and fold it over. Stick in the skewer to keep it closed. Carefully lift the chicken so that the other end, which is still open, is pointing upwards. Put the stuffing inside, filling and packing it in with the spoon. When it is full, fold over the skin flap and stick in another skewer to hold it shut.

6 Put the butter into the pot and place it on a low heat until the butter melts. Carefully place the chicken into the melted butter using the two carving forks.

7 Turn up the heat until the chicken starts to sizzle. Let it cook for a minute and then turn the chicken on to its side with the carving forks until that starts to sizzle. Do this until all the chicken has been fried in the butter.

8 Lower the heat, add the onions and sprinkle the chicken with nutmeg and thyme. Add the teacup of hot water.

9 Turn the heat very low so that the water is just bubbling. Put the lid on the pot and cook for 2 hours.

(You can make some creamy mashed potatoes and spinach to eat with the chicken while it is cooking. Use frozen spinach and follow the cooking instructions on the packet. When it is cooked stir in a knob of butter and a pinch of nutmeg. You'll find a good recipe for mashed potatoes on page 47.)

10 Wash and dry the large plate and lay it beside the hob.

11 After the 2 hours are over, remove the pot from the heat and place on a heat-resistant surface.

12 Take the chicken out of the pot using the carving forks and lay it on the plate. Keep the liquid that you have cooked the chicken in to make the gravy. Ask an adult to remove the skewers and carve the chicken.

13 Now you can either make the gravy or you can try the recipe for Drappit Eggs (the recipes are opposite).

14 When the gravy and eggs are ready, place a slice of breast and dark meat, and a spoonful of the stuffing from inside the chicken on to each plate. Serve with the potatoes, spinach, eggs and gravy – everyone will enjoy this lovely meal.

To make the gravy

1 Turn up the heat under the pot and let the liquid in the pot (this is called 'stock') boil for 5 minutes until it becomes thicker.

2 Turn down the heat and taste the stock. Add some salt and pepper if you think it needs it.

3 The gravy is now ready. Carefully pour it into a gravy boat or jug.

To make Drappit Eggs

Drappit Eggs are poached eggs and it was traditional to serve them with Howtowdie.

1 Collect 6 eggs and a teacup.

2 Add two cups of water to the stock in the pot and turn up the heat until the stock is just bubbling.

3 Break an egg into the cup and gently pour it into the pot. Do this with the other 5 eggs.

4 Turn the heat very low and cook the eggs for about 3 minutes.

5 Turn off the heat and remove each egg from the pot with a draining spoon. Place them on to each person's plate of chicken and stuffing.

6 Taste the stock left in the pot and add salt and pepper if you think it needs it. Pour the stock into a jug or gravy boat to serve as gravy with your meal.

Stoved Grouse

This is the way they cooked grouse in Argyll which is in the west of Scotland. You can use poussins (very small chickens) instead of grouse, if you wish.

Adv

Serves 2

2 hrs

Cook ∭

Hob ◎

E. Wok ○

E. Fry ❖

70

HAVE READY

a brace of grouse (2 oven-ready birds)

225g (8oz) potatoes – peeled and cut into chips

1 teaspoon of sugar

1 tablespoon bacon fat or cooking oil

a green salad of lettuce, cucumber and celery

rowan jelly or cranberry sauce

salt + pepper

large soup pot with tight-fitting lid

large plate

sharp knife

chopping board

clean tea towel

pair of tongs

bowl

draining spoon

wooden spoon

tablespoon

teaspoon

TO MAKE

1 Wash the grouse well by holding them under a cold running tap and letting the water run through and over them. Drain the water out of them and dry them with a clean tea towel.

2 Put the bacon fat or oil into the pot and place it on the cooker. Turn on the heat and add the sugar.

3 Stir in the sugar with the wooden spoon. When the oil and sugar are hot, carefully place the grouse in the pot.

4 Fry one side of the grouse and then turn them with the tongs to do the other side. Keep turning until the outside is all browned. Turn them on their bottoms and turn the heat very low.

5 Put the lid on the pot and leave the grouse to cook for 1 hour.

6 After this time take off the lid and put the potatoes in the pot around the grouse. Sprinkle them with salt and pepper.

7 Put the lid back on the pot and cook for 30 minutes.

8 While the grouse are cooking, prepare the salad: break off the lettuce leaves and wash them under cold running water. Shake dry. Wash the celery and cucumber and place them on the chopping board. Cut them into thin slices and put them in the bowl with the lettuce. (You'll find a recipe for salad dressing on page 22.)

9   Set the table with knives, forks, the green salad and rowan jelly or cranberry sauce. Remember to set out napkins and a finger bowl for each person – your fingers are the only things to use to attack the bones!

10 After the grouse and potatoes have cooked for 30 minutes, turn off the heat.

11 Lift the grouse out of the pot using the draining spoon and tongs and place on the plate.

12 Use the draining spoon to lift out the potatoes and place them around the grouse.

13 Add a little water to the juices left in the pot and turn on the heat again. Boil the juices a little to make some gravy. When the gravy has thickened, dip a spoon into the pan and drop a little of the gravy on to a teaspoon. Wait until it has cooled before you taste it and add some salt if you think it needs it. Pour into a jug or gravy boat.

14 Dish the grouse and potatoes on to each person's plate. Now try your very first taste of grouse – they are fun to eat.

Roast Pheasant

Roast Pheasant was traditionally decorated with the tail feathers stuck into the tail end after the bird was cooked. Resting on a silver ashet, it was carried to the table to be carved by the man of the household.

W W W

Adv

Serves 4

1hr 30 mins

Finish the dish with bread sauce, potatoes and green salad

Cook ≋

Oven ☐

Freeze ✳

HAVE READY

one young cock pheasant – ready to cook

225g (8oz) streaky bacon

25g (1oz) butter

salt + pepper

roasting tin

saucepan

clean tea towel

large plate

aluminium foil

2 carving forks

sieve

tongs

skewer

teacup

oven gloves

TO MAKE

1 Arrange the shelves in the oven so that the roasting tin will fit into the middle. Heat the oven at Gas 4, 350°F or 180°C.

2 Wash the pheasant by holding the open body under a cold running tap and allow the water to run over and through the pheasant. Wipe dry with a clean tea towel.

3 Place half the butter inside the body cavity – this is to keep the flesh moist.

4 Rub the rest of the butter over the pheasant.

5 Place the pheasant in the roasting tin and sprinkle with a little salt. Lay the rashers of bacon one by one on top of the breast until it is covered.

6 Cover the whole tin with aluminium foil – like making a tent over the pheasant. Fold the foil over and under the edge of the tin.

7 Place the tin on the middle shelf of the oven and cook for 45–60 minutes, depending on the size of the pheasant.

8 Remove the tin from the oven, using oven gloves, and open the foil. Be careful to avoid the steam which will escape from the foil. Test the pheasant by sticking the pointed end of a skewer into the breast. If it feels tender and a little clear juice runs out, the pheasant is ready.

9 Turn up the oven heat to Gas 7, 425°F or 220°C. Use the oven gloves to remove the foil from the tin (watch out for the steam). Lift the bacon off the pheasant with a fork.

10 Carefully use the oven gloves to place the bird back in the oven to brown. This takes 10 minutes.

11 Take the tin out of the oven and set on a heat-resistant surface.

12 Use the carving forks to place the pheasant on to the large plate.

13 To make the gravy pour 1 teacup of cold water into the tin. The fat will become solid. Pour the mixture through a sieve into the saucepan – the fat will stay in the sieve. Make sure you scrape all the juices out of the tin.

14 Heat the liquid in the pan until it boils. Boil for 5 minutes and add a little salt and pepper. Taste and add more salt and pepper if you think it needs it. Now you have made the gravy, pour it into a jug.

15 Ask an adult to carve the pheasant. Serve with the gravy.

It is traditional to eat roast pheasant with clear gravy, browned breadcrumbs, green salad with watercress, bread sauce, game chip potatoes and redcurrant or rowan jelly.

Browned Crumbs

10 mins

Cook 〰

Hob ◎

HAVE READY

50g (2oz) fresh breadcrumbs

25g (1oz) butter

saucepan

wooden spoon

TO MAKE

1 Put the butter in the pan and place it on the heat to melt.

2 Pour in the crumbs and keep stirring with the wooden spoon until the crumbs turn golden brown in colour. Switch off the heat.

3 Pour into a dish and they are ready to eat.

Green Salad

You can now buy a mixture of lettuces ready prepared. Put them in a bowl with some chopped celery, sliced cucumber and watercress for an easy salad. (There is a recipe for salad dressing on page 22.)

Bread Sauce

40 mins

Cook 〰

Hob ◎

HAVE READY

small onion

24 whole cloves

275ml (½ pint) milk

50g (2oz) fresh white breadcrumbs

saucepan

wooden spoon

draining spoon

TO MAKE

1 Peel the onion and stick the cloves into it. Place the onion into the pan and pour the milk over it.

2 Put the pan on a low heat for 30 minutes. The flavour of the onion will go into the milk – this is called an 'infusion'.

3 Remove the onion from the milk with the draining spoon and throw it away.

4 Pour the breadcrumbs into the milk in the pan. Turn up the heat to medium and keep stirring until the sauce thickens and starts to bubble. Add more milk if the sauce is too thick.

5 Taste the sauce and add some salt and pepper until you like the flavour. Pour the sauce into a bowl and serve hot.

Game Chip Potatoes

5 mins

Cook 〰

Oven ☐

HAVE READY

2 pkts plain crisps

1 baking tray

TO MAKE

1 Heat the oven to Gas 6, 400°F or 200°C.

2 Empty the crisps on to the baking tray.

3 Use the oven gloves to put the tray into the oven. Heat for 4 to 5 minutes.

4 Use the oven gloves to take the tray out of the oven and pour the crisps into a dish. Now they are ready to eat.

Salmi of Pheasant

This recipe was used in the large game lodges where there were often too many roasted pheasants. If you wish, you can use chicken or turkey instead.

HAVE READY

450g (1lb) cooked pheasant, chicken or turkey

570ml (1 pint) gravy – use gravy mix or granules

110g (4oz) mushrooms – peeled and chopped

saucepan

casserole dish with lid

clean tea towel

sharp knife

chopping board

wooden spoon

TO MAKE

1 Adjust the shelves in the oven so that the casserole will sit on the middle one. Heat the oven to Gas 4, 350°F or 180°C.

2 Make one pint of gravy in the pan following the recipe on the packet.

3 Wash the mushrooms under cold running water and dry them with the clean tea towel. Place them on the chopping board and cut into quarters with the sharp knife. Put in the casserole dish.

4 Put the cooked meat on to the chopping board and cut into large chunks (about 4cm square) with the sharp knife. Put the pieces into the casserole along with the mushrooms.

5 Pour the gravy over and stir together with the wooden spoon. Put on the lid.

6 Use the oven gloves to place the casserole in the oven. Cook for 45 minutes.

7 While the casserole is cooking, boil some rice to eat with the salmi.

8 After 45 minutes turn off the oven. Using the oven gloves and being very careful, take the dish out of the oven and put it on a heat-resistant surface.

9 Set the table – dinner is ready to serve!

Inter

Serves 4

1 hr

Finish the dish with boiled rice

Cook 〰

Oven ▢

Freeze ✳

Stewed Rabbit

Stewed Rabbit was a very popular dish throughout Scotland – there were lots of wild rabbits and they were easy to catch! You can cook chicken portions, thighs and drumsticks in the same way.

🍞 🍞 🍞

Adv

Serves 4

2 hrs

Finish the dish with peas and new potatoes

Cook ∭

Hob ◎

E. Wok ◑

E. Fry ❖

Freeze ✳

HAVE READY

I rabbit – skinned and jointed

I onion – peeled and chopped

I apple – peeled, cored and sliced

100g (4oz) bacon – chopped

I tablespoon cooking oil

2 tablespoons flour

I teaspoon salt

¼ teaspoon pepper

boiling water

stew pan with lid

large polythene bag

serving dish (pie dish or casserole)

plate

sharp knife

chopping board

pair cooking tongs

draining spoon

wooden spoon

tablespoon

teaspoon

TO MAKE

1 Mix the flour, salt and pepper together in the polythene bag.

2 Add the rabbit joints to the bag. Tie the top of the bag or hold the open end tightly shut and shake well to coat all of the rabbit with the flour mixture. Take the rabbit out of the bag, shake off the extra flour and put it on to the plate.

3 Put the oil into the stew pan, place on the hob and turn on the heat to medium to heat the oil.

4 Add the rabbit and use the wooden spoon to keep turning the rabbit until all the meat has turned brown – this is called 'browning'.

5 Add the chopped onions and stir well.

6 Add the apple and pour in enough boiling water to come halfway up the meat. Boil for 5 minutes.

7 Turn down the heat so that the water is just bubbling. Cover with the lid and cook for 1 hour, stirring occasionally.

8 Take off the lid and stir in the chopped bacon. Put the lid back on and cook for another 30 minutes.

While the stew is cooking, why not boil some new potatoes and garden peas to eat with your stew.

9 When the 30 minutes are up, take off the lid and taste the gravy. Add some more salt and pepper if you think it needs it. Turn off the heat.

10 Carefully, using the tongs, lift the pieces of rabbit on to the serving dish. Lift out the apple and bacon with the draining spoon and place them over the rabbit.

11 Carefully pour the gravy into a jug to serve with the rabbit.

12 Put some stew, boiled new potatoes and peas on to your plate and imagine that you are sitting in a cottage hundreds of years ago, eating your meal in front of a crackling fire and listening to your father talking about his day's work on the farm!

Highland Hare Cakes

In earlier times hares were eaten quite often and included in the daily diet, just as we might eat sausages today. The time to eat fresh hares is from September until March, unlike rabbits which can be eaten at any time of the year. Hare meat is darker and has a much stronger flavour than rabbit meat. You can use minced turkey, venison, beef, or lamb instead of hare meat for this recipe.

Inter

Serves 4

30 mins

Finish the dish with baked potatoes and vegetables

Cook 〰

Hob ◎

E. Fry ❖

Freeze ❋

78

HAVE READY

225g (8oz) minced hare meat

110g (4oz) minced bacon

half an onion – peeled and finely chopped

1 egg

2 slices stale bread

1 teaspoon mushroom ketchup or HP sauce

½ teaspoon celery salt

½ teaspoon salt

fish dressing

cooking oil

frying pan

mixing bowl

small bowl

teacup

kitchen towel

small sieve

plate

tongs

fork

dessertspoon

teaspoon

TO MAKE

1 Put the stale bread into the small bowl and cover with cold water to make it soft – this is called 'soaking'.

2 Break the egg into the teacup and beat well.

3 Mix the minced hare and bacon, celery salt and sauce in the mixing bowl.

4 Add the egg and mix well.

5 Pour the bread and water into a sieve and let the water run down the sink. Put the bread into the mixing bowl.

6 Add the salt and use the fork to mix everything well together.

7 Wash and dry your hands. Divide the mixture into four equal portions. Using your hands, make each portion of the mixture into a round flat cake about 3cm thick and put them on the plate.

8 Tear off a piece of kitchen towel and shake about 2 tablespoons of fish dressing on to the middle.

9 Place a meat cake into the crumbs and turn it in the crumbs to make sure it is all covered. Do this with all the cakes and put them on the plate.

10 Pour 2 tablespoons of cooking oil into the frying pan and put it on the hob. Turn on the heat to medium. The fat is hot enough to cook when a piece of dry bread dropped in the pan begins to sizzle.

11 Fry the meat cakes until they are golden on each side, use the tongs to turn them. Always be careful when you are frying as the oil is very hot.

12 Wash and dry the plate and cover it with a double layer of paper towel. When the Hare Cakes are cooked, use the tongs to lift them out of the pan and on to the plate to drain.

13 You can eat hot Highland Hare Cakes in a bread roll with salad or with baked jacket potatoes, broccoli and carrot sticks. Can you think of another way you would like to eat them?

Venison Pasties

This is a simple version of the traditional recipe which was described by Sir Walter Scott in his novel *Old Mortality* as 'the Princely Venison Pasty'. Venison pasties make a tasty snack. They can be eaten hot or cold and they are nice for a picnic or as something different for your packed lunch at school.

Inter

Makes 4 pasties

1 hr

Cook ♒

Oven ☐

Freeze ✳

Have Ready

340g (12oz) ready-made shortcrust pastry

225g (8oz) cooked Gillie's Venison (page 82)

1 small egg

flour to roll out the pastry

a little cooking oil

baking tray

rolling pin

plate

pastry brush

palette knife or fish slice

small bowl

sharp knife

saucer

knife + fork

oven gloves

To Make

1   Turn on the oven and heat at Gas 7, 425°F or 220°C.

2   Wash and dry the kitchen table or worktop. Dust some flour on to the worktop and on to the rolling pin. Place the pastry on the floured top and roll it out to the thickness of a china plate.

3   Place a saucer upside down on top of the pastry and cut round it with a knife. Cut out 4 circles like this. Roll the scraps into a ball and put it into a plastic bag – you can use this again.

4   Divide the cooked venison into 4 equal portions and place in the centre of each circle of pastry.

5   Brush round the edges of the pastry with the pastry brush dipped in cold water.

6   Lift the edges of the pastry up over the top of the meat to make a semi-circle. Press the edges together with your thumb and fingers to make sure that the pasty is sealed.

7   Using the point of the sharp knife, make a small slit in the top of each pasty. This allows the steam to escape and helps to make the pastry crispy.

8 Using a piece of kitchen towel, rub a little oil over the surface of the baking tray. Lay the four pasties on the tray.

9 Break the egg into a small bowl and beat it with a fork. Paint some of the egg over the top of the pasties with the pastry brush. This is called an 'egg wash' and it gives the pastry a shiny, golden crisp skin when it is cooked.

10 Use the oven gloves to put the tray into the oven on a shelf near the top. Cook for 15 to 20 minutes. If the pasties are still not golden brown, leave them for another 5 minutes.

11 Remove the hot tray from the oven using the oven gloves. Put the tray down on a heat-resistant surface and lift the pasties on to a plate using either a fish slice or the palette knife.

12 Serve hot with potatoes or chips and vegetables, or cold as a tasty snack. Perhaps baked beans would be good to eat with your Vension Pasties? What would you like to try?

Gillie's Venison

A 'Gillie' is a guide and helper for people who are either hunting or fishing in the Highlands. The Gillies sheltered in a place called a 'bothy' where they would normally only have an open fire and a pan to cook in.

Inter

Serves 4

1 hr 30 mins

Finish the dish with baked potatoes

Cook ∭

Hob ◎

E. Wok ○

E. Fry ❖

Freeze ❋

82

HAVE READY

450g (1lb) lean shoulder of venison (you can use frozen, diced venison)

25g (1oz) bacon fat, dripping, or cooking oil

some plain flour

some water

1 teaspoon salt

pinch pepper

stew pan with tight-fitting lid

medium-sized polythene bag

large plate

sharp knife

chopping board

wooden spoon

tablespoon

draining spoon

TO MAKE

1 Cut the venison into pieces about 2cm.

2 Mix 1 tablespoon of flour with the salt and pepper in the polythene bag. Put the meat into the bag, tie up the open end and shake until the meat is coated in flour.

3 Put the bacon fat, dripping or cooking oil into the pan and place on a medium heat to melt the fat.

4 Place the venison into the pan and stir with the wooden spoon until the meat is brown all over.

5 Lower the heat, sprinkle with salt and pepper and put the lid on the pan. Cook on a low heat for 1 hour.

6 Use the draining spoon to lift the meat out of the pan on to the large plate. Drain off the fat from the pan, leaving the juices. (The fat will float on top of the juices and can be lifted off with a tablespoon.)

7 Put 2 teaspoons of flour into the pan and stir into the juices with a wooden spoon. While you are stirring, slowly and carefully pour in some water until the mixture is like gravy. Turn up the heat a little until the gravy bubbles and boils.

8 Turn off the heat and taste the gravy. Add some more salt and pepper until you like the flavour. Pour over the meat.

9 Serve Gillie's Venison with baked potatoes.

Oatmeal

'May the mouse ne'er leave yer Girnel [meal chest or store] wi a tear in his ee!'.
This was a common toast to wish you enough to eat all the days of your life.
Oats used to be the staple grain in Highland Scotland. Once the oats were
harvested they were prepared for use by a process called 'dressing'. One method was
called 'gradan', which comes from the Irish word grad, meaning 'quick'. This involved
taking a handful of oats in one hand, setting the ears alight and, while they were
burning, beating off the grain with a stick. The grain was then 'winnowed' (the lighter
chaff was blown away), ground and baked.

The oats were ground into oatmeal using a hand mill called a 'quern'. This was
simply two round stones set one on top of the other. The one on the top had a hole
in the middle through which the oats were poured. A wooden handle turned the
stones to grind the oats into meal which fell out from the sides of the stones into a
tray. The meal was then ground some more with a wooden spindle into coarse,
medium or fine texture, depending on the needs of the cook.

Oats were plentiful and cheap and so folk ate them at almost every meal. Students
at Scottish universities survived on almost nothing but oatmeal, and some Scottish
universities still celebrate an annual holiday called 'Mealy Monday'.

Oatmeal had plenty of uses apart from food. Before fridges were invented to help
keep meat fresh, it was completely covered in oatmeal. Every day the meat was taken
out, wiped and put back into the oatmeal where it was said to 'keep' for up to a
fortnight. Before the meat was cooked, it was soaked in fresh oatmeal and water to

remove any sour flavours. There was a special chest (called a 'girnel') full of meal which was used to store oatcakes, mealie puddings and cheeses. These stayed fresh as long as they were buried in the oatmeal.

Oatmeal was also used to make soap, and the water left after a muslin bag of oatmeal has been soaked in it is said to be very good for your complexion (the skin on your face).

Oatmeal was very important to Scottish folk – think of what Dr Johnson (a famous traveller and writer) once wrote: 'A grain, which in England is generally given to horses, but in Scotland supports the people.' The reply was: 'Yes sir, but where will you find such horses, or such people?'

Oats are very nutritious and are almost the perfect food, lacking only in vitamin C which we can get from eating fresh fruit and vegetables.

The Story of Crowdie or Fuarag

Crowdie is the Lowland name for a mixture of oatmeal and cold water or buttermilk, mixed to the consistency of double cream. It used to be eaten for breakfast all over Scotland – 'Crowdie-time' is an old name for breakfast.

Sour milk and oatmeal mixed together was known as 'Cauld Steer' and a special Crowdie, called 'Meal and Ale', was made to celebrate harvest. In this recipe ale and oatmeal were stirred together with treacle and whisky. The mixture was left to stand all day before the party. Usually a ring had been put into the mixture – whoever found the ring was said to be the first to get married.

In the Highlands, the mixture of oatmeal and water or buttermilk is called 'Drammoch', 'Fuarag' or 'Stapag', and Crowdie is the name given to a cream cheese made from fresh milk.

'Crowdie' comes from the Gaelic word *cruaidh*, which means thick and firm.

White or Mealie Puddings

Mealie Puddings are made from a mixture of oatmeal, salt, suet, onions, and allspice. Allspice is also called Jamaica pepper and is made by grinding the ripe, dried berries of a myrtle tree, which grows in Jamaica. The pudding mixture is put into skins and looks like large sausages. Then it is steamed for about an hour. Traditionally, the Mealie Puddings were hung up to dry or kept buried in the oatmeal in the meal chest or 'girnel' so that they would keep fresh.

In the eighteenth century the taverns of Edinburgh were very popular. Some of them were run by women who were called 'Luckies'. Each Luckie had a 'speciality of the house' and Pudding Lizzie's tavern at Jock's Lodge was famous for her Mealie Puddings which one customer said were 'Braw healthy eatin!'

You you can still buy Mealie Puddings from the butcher or supermarket today; even chip shops serve them ready cooked.

HAVE READY

one pudding per person	saucepan
water	knife
	fork
	draining spoon
	plate

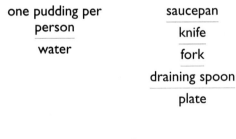

TO MAKE

1 Prick the skin of the puddings with the fork to stop it from bursting. Wash and dry the fork.

2 Place the puddings in the pan and cover with boiling water.

3 Put the pan on a medium heat and cook for 5 to 10 minutes, depending on the size of the Mealie Puddings.

4 Take the pan off the heat and place on a heat-resistant surface. Use a draining spoon to remove the puddings from the water and put them on the plate.

5 Hold the Mealie Pudding with the fork and use the knife to cut along its length. Do the same with each pudding, then they are ready to eat.

6 Serve Mealie Puddings on their own, or with stew, mince, roasts, gravy, potatoes and vegetables – anything you like!

Simple

Serve one pudding per person

10 mins

Cook ∭

Hob ◎

E. Wok ○

Porridge

People spoke of Porridge as 'Them' and it was traditional to eat 'Them' standing up. No one really knows the reason why, but it could be that they believed they could eat more Porridge that way!

Porridge was served in wooden 'bickers' called 'luggies'. These had two handles, with deep, straight sides. Often the luggies had a double bottom containing a dry pea which was rattled to ask for a second helping! It was traditional to stir Porridge in a clockwise direction, using a straight wooden stick called a 'spurtle' or 'theevil'.

Porridge has many different names: it is called 'Milgruel' in Shetland; 'Brochan' in the Highlands; 'Gogar' in the Borders; and in the east of Scotland people call it 'Bluthrie'. Everyone had their own particular way to make Porridge and here is a simple one.

Inter

Serves 2

1 hr

Finish the dish with fresh cold milk

Cook 〰

Hob ◎

E. Wok ○

E. Fry ✣

86

HAVE READY

50g (2oz) medium oatmeal	saucepan
570ml (½ pint) water	2 bowls
½ teaspoon salt	teacup
cold, creamy milk	wooden spoon or spurtle
	measuring jug
	saucer
	teaspoon

TO MAKE

1 Pour the water into the pan, place on the heat and boil the water.

2 When the water is boiling, turn down the heat until it is just bubbling. Hold the pan handle with one hand and stir the water with the wooden spoon or spurtle.

3 Sprinkle the oatmeal into the pan from the teacup and stir rapidly. Be careful not to splash yourself. The porridge should become like thick double cream. If it is not thick enough, add a little more oatmeal, and if it's too thick add more water. (The way that oatmeal cooks varies depending on where it was grown and if it is ground fine, medium, rough or pinhead.)

4 Try to keep stirring until there are no lumps – some people like the lumps. Leave them if you do.

5 Turn down the heat to very low. Remove the spoon, rest it on a saucer and put the lid on the pan. Cook for 10 minutes and then add the salt. (Porridge needs to be cooked with salt but, if you add it at the beginning, it will make the oatmeal hard; it will stop swelling and so the porridge will not be thick and creamy.)

6 Cook for another 30 minutes with the lid on. Stir it from time to time to stop the porridge sticking.

7 The traditional way to serve porridge is in a soup bowl with a separate small bowl of creamy milk for each person. First take a hot spoon of porridge, dip it into the cold, creamy milk and pop it in your mouth – mmmm! Some people like to put toppings on their porridge: sugar, honey, syrup, raw oatmeal, wheatgerm – take your pick!

A faster way of making oatmeal porridge is to soak the oatmeal and water overnight in the pan.

Place the water and oatmeal in the pan and leave overnight.

1 In the morning, turn on the heat under the pan. Keep stirring as the porridge heats and thickens.

2 When it starts to boil, cook for 15 minutes and then add the salt. Turn down the heat to very low.

3 Cook for another 15 minutes with the lid on. Stir it from time to time to stop the porridge sticking.

4 Spoon into a bowl and serve with a separate bowl of fresh cold milk.

The Story of a Fitless Cock

In the eighteenth century cock fights were held in the parish schools to celebrate the festival of Fastern's E'n (the night before the first day of Lent). It was traditional to cook and eat a 'fitless', 'feisty' or 'fastyn' cock on that night.
This dish is made of oatmeal, suet, salt, pepper and chopped onions mixed together with egg. The mixture is then made into the shape of a chicken and boiled in a cloth (known as a 'clout') like a dumpling.

Oatmeal (Aigar) Brose

Brose is a porridge which is made by adding a boiling liquid to meal, usually oatmeal. There are many different types: Brose without butter is called 'Blind Brose'. 'Milk Madlocks' is Brose made with hot milk instead of boiling water. 'Pot Brose' is made by throwing handfuls of oatmeal into boiling milk in a pan and cooking it for a few minutes. Aigar Brose is another version: if you like it why not try all the other kinds?

Brose is traditionally served with a separate bowl of buttermilk for each person. You take a spoonful of brose, dip it into the bowl of buttermilk and then eat it. This means that the cold buttermilk does not cool the brose in the bowl. Buttermilk was known as 'soor dook' and a cart (called the 'soor dook cart') came round folk's houses selling it by the jugful from a big churn.

HAVE READY

50g (2oz) medium oatmeal

12g (½oz) butter

boiling water

1 teaspoon salt

bowl

wooden spoon (or spurtle)

TO MAKE

1 Put the oatmeal into the bowl. Add the butter and salt.

2 Pour enough boiling water into the bowl to cover the oatmeal.

3 Either use the spurtle or hold the wooden spoon upside down and stir the mixture with the handle! This will help to make lumps or 'knotty tams', as they were called. If you prefer Brose without lumps, stir it with the spoon in the usual way.

4 Serve the Brose hot in a bowl with another bowl full of fresh cold milk or buttermilk. Try it, it is very good for you.

The Story of Sowans

In the days when the farmers sent their oats to the mill nearby, the ground oats were returned to the farmer along with a bag of the inner husks of the oat grain. These are called 'sids', and a lot of the good food value of oats is in these husks. The sids were made into a kind of smooth porridge pudding called Sowans.
Sowans were made by the Celts hundreds of years ago and the name is from the Gaelic word sughan ('soo-an'). Christmas Eve, called Sowans Nicht, was when friends all got together to share a large bowl of Sowans. At Hallowe'en Sowans were cooked with butter and a ring was hidden in the bowl. It was thought that the person who found the ring would be the first to marry.
The Sowans were made in a special barrel called a 'Sowan Bowie'. The sids were put into the bowie, covered with warm water and left to go sour. Then the water and sids were poured through a sieve (called a 'sye') into a wide container – this was called 'syein o the so'ons'. The sids were thrown away.
The liquid in the container was left to stand for two days until all the heavy, starchy stuff had sunk to the bottom. When the Sowans was needed, the clear liquid was poured off the top and the sediment (the stuff which had sunk to the bottom) was boiled with a little salt and water to make a smooth creamy porridge. It was eaten from bowls with cream and said to be very good for you. Physicians prescribed Sowans for patients with indigestion!

The Story of Atholl Brose

Atholl Brose is actually another kind of Crowdie because it too is made with a cold, not hot, liquid (Brose is usually made with a hot liquid). The first time we know it was drunk was in 1475 when it was used in the capture of the Lord of the Isles by the clan Murray. The Lord of the Isles, who was hiding from his enemies, drank from a small well in a rock every day. When the Earl of Atholl, chief of the clan Murray, heard about this, he told his men to put a mixture of run honey (honey from the comb), oatmeal and whisky into the well. The Lord of the Isles was so pleased with the wonderful drink that he stayed too long at the well and was captured by Atholl and his men.
Now there are many recipes for Atholl Brose: some use honey to sweeten it, and in others whipped cream and toasted oatmeal are mixed with the whisky.

CREAM

Gruel

Gruel is called 'water-berry' in Dumfriesshire.
Lots of different flavours were added to Gruel, like fruit, wine, sugar, honey
or butter. You can add anything you like — what others can you think of?
Sometimes folk let the Gruel cool and set like jelly, then they spread it on
toast or bread.

Inter

Serves 1

50 mins

Cook

Hob

E. Wok

E. Fry

HAVE READY

1 tablespoon fine
oatmeal

275ml (½ pint) water

½ teaspoon salt (or
sugar or honey)

saucepan

measuring jug

bowl

sieve

wooden spoon

tablespoon

teaspoon

TO MAKE

1 Put the oatmeal and salt into the bowl and cover with the water.

2 Leave to soak for 30 minutes, stirring occasionally with the wooden spoon.

3 Put the sieve over the pan and carefully pour the oatmeal and water through the sieve into the pan.

4 Put the pan on the cooker and turn on the heat to medium.

5 Hold the handle of the pan in one hand and use the other hand to stir the gruel with the wooden spoon until it is boiling.

6 Turn down the heat until the mixture is just bubbling and cook for 15 minutes, stirring occasionally.

7 Pour into a mug, add a little milk to cool it down and there you have Gruel — it makes a great change from cuppa-soup!

Hodgils

This recipe comes from the Borders. Hodgils are small tasty dumplings which were cooked in soup. When there is a nice pot of soup cooking it is easy to make these dumplings to cook in it. They make the soup more interesting!

HAVE READY

50g (2oz) oatmeal	plate
teacup of soup	bowl
small bunch of chives	pair kitchen scissors
½ teaspoon salt	ladle
pinch pepper	wooden spoon
	2 dessert spoons
	teaspoon

TO MAKE

1　Put the oatmeal, salt and pepper into the bowl.

2　Wash the chives under cold running water. Hold them over the bowl and snip them into small pieces with the scissors.

3　Use the ladle to spoon out some of the soup into a cup.

4　Using one of the dessert spoons, slowly add the liquid to the bowl and stir it into the oatmeal mixture. Do this until you have a soft dough (like soft play dough).

5　Take both of the dessert spoons and lift a small piece of dough on to one spoon. Use the other spoon to push it off on to the plate to make a small dumpling. Repeat this until all the dough is used up. You can make them as large or small as you like.

6　Carefully drop your Hodgils into the boiling soup 20 minutes before it is ready. Put the lid on the pan and leave them to cook with the soup.

7　When the soup is ready, serve it in bowls with the dumplings floating on top – a surprise for the family!

Simple

Needs liquid from cooking soup

Makes 8 small dumplings

30 mins

Cook ≈

Hob ◎

E. Wok ○

E. Fry ❖

Carcakes or Oatmeal Fritters

Carcakes are a kind of oatcake eaten at breakfast time – they are delicious with bacon!

HAVE READY

110g (4oz) oatmeal	frying pan
some milk	large plate
some oil to fry	bowl
pinch bicarbonate of soda	wooden spoon
pinch cream of tartar	fish slice
pinch salt	kitchen towel
pinch pepper	tablespoon

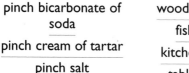

TO MAKE

1 Put the oatmeal, bicarbonate of soda, cream of tartar, salt and pepper into the bowl. (A pinch is the amount you can hold between your thumb and index finger.)

2 Use the wooden spoon to stir in enough milk to make the mixture like thick pouring cream.

3 Place the frying pan on the cooker and pour in enough oil to cover the bottom.

4 Turn on the heat under the pan and heat the oil. (Test it by dropping a small piece of dry bread into the oil. If the bread sizzles and turns brown, the oil is ready.)

5 Drop in some tablespoons of the oatmeal mixture (this is called batter), cook for a few minutes and then turn them with the fish slice to brown both sides.

6 Use the fish slice to remove them from the pan and lay them on a plate covered with kitchen towel to drain off the oil (this makes them healthier to eat).

7 Eat them hot with crispy bacon at breakfast time or as a snack for lunch. Ask your friends to join you for something a bit different to eat.

Puddings and Desserts

Many years ago Scotland and France were both enemies of England and so they decided to to help one another in their battles – this was called 'the Auld Alliance'. Through this Alliance, the two countries also traded together and many French ideas, including recipes, found their way to Scotland. 'Dessert' is a French word.

Desserts and puddings were first introduced to Scotland in the 1500s. It was the custom that the guests would eat the the main part of their meal at one table and then move to another room to enjoy the desserts and puddings laid out there. When King James VI of Scotland visited New College, St Andrews, he was served a 'banquet of wat and dry confectiones, with all sorts of wyne' which he enjoyed so much he stayed a 'guid whyll'.

Many of these early desserts were made from a mixture of cream and oatmeal. However, only royalty, nobility and the upper classes ate them regularly. The ordinary folk only ate puddings at special occasions and celebrations and it was two or three hundred years later that puddings were eaten more often.

Scottish Summer Salad

The counties of Fife and Angus are famous for their strawberries, raspberries, and red and black currants.

Inter

Needs left for
2 hrs

Serves 6

15 mins

Cook ≋

Hob ◎

E. Wok ○

E. Fry ❖

94

HAVE READY

900g (2lb) fresh fruit – a mixture of raspberries, strawberries, black and red currants

225g (8oz) sugar

570ml (1 pint) water

juice of 1 lemon, or 1 tablespoon Jiff lemon

12g (½oz) split almonds

stew pan

timer

pair small scissors

pair sugar tongs or tweezers

colander

large bowl

wooden spoon

tablespoon

TO MAKE

1 Put the water and sugar in the pan and stir to dissolve the sugar.

2 Place the pan on the hob and turn on the heat to medium. Bring the sugar and water in the pan to the boil (it begins to bubble in the pan). Boil for 15 minutes. Be careful as the steam coming from the pan is very hot and can burn you. Also, make sure that the handle of the pan is not sticking out from the hob.

3 While the sugar and water are boiling you can prepare the fruit. Set the timer for 15 minutes so you don't forget about the boiling liquid while you are busy with the fruit.

4 Raspberries – remove all the green leaves and hard centres. Hold the stalk between your thumb and index finger: it should pull out very easily. Do this with all the raspberries. Put them in the colander and wash under cold running water. Let the water drain out of them and put them in the large bowl.

5 Strawberries – use the sugar tongs to pull out the stock and hard core from the berry. Put it in the colander. Do this with all the strawberries and wash them under cold running water. Let the water drain out and then put the strawberries in the bowl.

6 Black and red currants – use the small scissors to snip the stalk and rough brown tip from each berry. This is called 'topping and tailing' the berries. Put them in the colander and wash them under cold running water. Let the water drain out and then put them in the bowl.

7 After 15 minutes turn off the heat under the pan and add the lemon juice.

8 Put all the fruit back in the colander in the sink to make sure that all the water is drained out.

9 Use the tablespoon to spoon all the fruit into the pan of syrup. Stir gently with the wooden spoon to cover the fruit.

10 Wash and dry the large bowl. Use the ladle to spoon the fruit salad from the pan into the bowl. Sprinkle the almonds on top.

11 Leave in a cool place for 2 hours for all the flavours to mix (this is called an 'infusion'). If you can, leave the fruit salad overnight.

12 Delicious! Why not have a real traditional Scottish summer pudding? Simply serve your Scottish Summer Salad with Hattit Kit (page 98) or Fuarag (page 96)!

Fuarag

Fuarag originally came from the Hebrides (islands off the west coast of Scotland). It can be eaten in two ways: as a dessert with some fruit, like raspberries or brambles, or as a kind of sweet cheese spread on oatcakes, biscuits or scones.

♕

Simple

Needs to chill
for 4 hrs

Serves 4

15 mins

Finish the dish
with fruit, bread
or oatcakes

Cook ∭

Grill ⌘

HAVE READY

50g (2oz) medium oatmeal

275g (½ pint) soured cream

1 tablespoon caster sugar

baking tray

bowl

wooden spoon

tablespoon

teaspoon

oven gloves

TO MAKE

1 Turn on the grill to medium. Pour the oatmeal on to the baking tray and spread it out evenly with the tablespoon.

2 Use the oven gloves to set the tray under the heated grill. Leave for a few moments to toast (it should turn a golden brown). Watch it all the time as oatmeal burns very easily.

3 Use the oven gloves to take the baking tray out from under the grill and set it on a heat-resistant surface.

4 Put the soured cream into the bowl and add the oatmeal. Stir it together with the wooden spoon.

5 Add the sugar and stir it again. Use the clean teaspoon to taste the sweetness. Add more sugar if you would like it to taste sweeter.

6 Leave in the fridge for as long as you can for the oatmeal to swell and thicken. Overnight is best.

7 Serve after your main meal or as a snack. Do you like it better than ice-cream?

Greiseagan

This is like a sweet Skirlie. The original recipe was made in the Hebrides and used small black berries, called 'bear-berries', which were found on the islands. This recipe uses currants and raisins instead, but you can make up your own recipe for Greiseagan by putting in your own choice of fruits – what about apricots and almonds?

HAVE READY

110g (4oz) medium oatmeal

110g (4oz) currants and raisins

50g (2oz) chopped suet

frying pan

2 wooden spoons

tablespoon

bowl

TO MAKE

1 Put the oatmeal, currants and raisins into the bowl. Stir them together with a wooden spoon.

2 Put the suet in the frying pan and place it on the cooker.

3 Turn on the heat and carefully fry the suet in the pan. Stir with the other wooden spoon until it is crisp.

4 Turn the heat to low and use the tablespoon to spoon the mixture of fruit and oatmeal into the pan. Stir everything together.

5 Cook for 5 minutes on a low heat, stirring to prevent the mixture from burning.

6 Now it is ready to eat. Serve in bowls with some cold, thick double cream or ice-cream . . . mmmmmmm!

Inter

Serves 4

25 mins

Finish the dish with cream or ice-cream

Cook ⌇

Hob ◎

E. Wok ○

E. Fry ❖

97

Hattit or Hatted Kit

This very old Highland recipe was made by milking the cow's milk into a pail of buttermilk (buttermilk is the part of the cream that is left after butter has been made from it). This made the milk go thick (this is called a 'curd'). The curd sat on the top and was called the 'hat'. Folk would make quite a lot of Hattit Kit as it kept for up two weeks in a cool place – you can do the same and keep it in the fridge.

🍳 Simple

Needs left for 36 hrs

Serves 4

25 mins

Cook ♒

Hob ◎

E. Wok ○

E. Fry ❖

HAVE READY

570ml (1 pint) buttermilk

275ml (½ pint) milk

150ml (¼ pint) double cream

50g (2oz) sugar

1 tablespoon rennet

grated nutmeg

saucepan

2 bowls

plate

whisk

sieve

wooden spoon

teaspoon

bowl scraper

TO MAKE

1 Pour the buttermilk and milk into the pan and put on the heat. Turn on the heat to low. Let the milk just get warm to blood heat (this is the temperature of our body so, when you dip a clean finger in the milk, it will feel neither hot nor cold). Do not allow the milk to get hot – if it is too hot the rennet, an enzyme which makes the curd, will not work.

2 Take the milk off the cooker and add the rennet. Pour it all into the bowl and cover with a plate. Leave overnight in a cool place (not in the fridge).

3 The next day there will be a curd on top of the milk in the bowl. Lay the sieve on top of the other bowl. Pour the set milk into the sieve, cover and leave to drain in a cool place for 24 hours. The curd will be left in the sieve.

4 Wash and dry the empty bowl. Scrape the stiff curd from the sieve into it.

5 Add 25g (1oz) sugar and a little nutmeg (enough to cover the tip of the teaspoon) to the curd and mix well together with the wooden spoon.

6   Taste with a clean teaspoon and add more nutmeg and sugar if you think it is needed.

7   Throw away the liquid which drained through the sieve and wash and dry the empty bowl.

8   Pour in the cream, 25g (1oz) sugar and a little nutmeg (the same amount as before: the tip of the teaspoon).

9   Lay the bowl on a damp cloth to stop it slipping and beat the cream with the whisk until it is stiff. (The cream is stiff when it stands up like mountain peaks. Be careful not to over whisk the cream or it will turn into butter.) Tap the whisk on the edge of the bowl to remove the cream.

10 Add the whipped cream to the curd and mix them gently together with the wooden spoon. Remove the spoon and chill in the fridge for 10 minutes before you eat it.

11 Hattit Kit tastes lovely on its own or with any kind of fruit. I think it's better than ice-cream!

Flummery

Inter

Needs left overnight

Must be eaten immediately

Serves 4

30 mins

Cook ≋

Hob ◎

E. Wok ○

E. Fry ❖

100

Flora McDonald is famous because she helped Bonnie Prince Charlie escape to the Isle of Skye in 1746 after the Battle of Culloden. This was when the Jacobites were beaten by the English Duke of Cumberland and his army near Inverness on Culloden Moor. Flora McDonald was arrested by the English halfway through eating a dish of Flummery!
Flummery has to be eaten immediately – puddings made to order!

HAVE READY

150ml (1 gill) milk

150ml (1 gill) double cream

150ml (1 gill) apple juice

3 egg yolks

75g (3oz) sugar

50g (2oz) currants

½ teaspoon ground nutmeg

saucepan (large enough for the mixing bowl to sit in without touching the bottom)

mixing bowl

small bowl

plate

whisk (electric or hand)

2 teacups

bowl scraper

sieve

tea towel

tablespoon

teaspoon

oven gloves

TO MAKE

Put the currants in the small bowl. Pour in the apple juice and cover the bowl with the plate. Leave overnight.

1 Carefully break an egg into the teacup. Make sure it is very fresh. Using one half of the eggshell, gently lift out the egg yolk and put it in the other teacup. Do the same with the other egg. (Save the egg whites – you can use them to make a meringue.)

2 Hold the sieve over the sink and pour the soaked currants into it to drain. Pour the currants back into the bowl.

3 Pour the pint of water into the saucepan, place it on the hob and heat until the water boils. Turn down the heat until the water is just moving in the pan.

4 Pour the milk and double cream into the mixing bowl and add the egg yolks, sugar and nutmeg. Use the oven gloves to place the mixing bowl in the pan of hot water.

5 Whisk until the mixture thickens and warms (5 minutes). Turn off the heat and carefully lift the bowl on to the folded tea towel using the oven gloves.

6 Spoon the mixture into four small bowls while it is hot. Sprinkle the toasted currants on top and eat straight away!

Morayshire Apples

Morayshire in the North East of Scotland is a rich farming area and is known as the 'Laich O'Moray'. The mild climate of the Moray Firth is perfect for growing apples and other fruit. This pudding is like a special apple crumble and is certainly very tasty.

HAVE READY

450g (1lb) stewed apples or 1 tin prepared apples

3oz granulated sugar

2 tablespoons water

pinch ground cloves

stew pan

2-pint pie dish

bowl

wooden spoon

tablespoon

oven gloves

TOPPING

110g (4oz) medium oatmeal

110g (4oz) soft brown sugar

50g (2oz) chopped suet

25g (1oz) chopped hazelnuts

TO MAKE

1 Arrange the shelves in the oven so that the pie dish will sit on the middle one. Turn on the oven to Gas 4, 350°F or 180°C.

2 Stew the apples (see page 6) and put them in the bottom of the pie dish. Sprinkle the granulated sugar and ground cloves over the top.

3 Now to make the topping. Use the wooden spoon to mix the oatmeal, suet, hazelnuts and half of the soft brown sugar together in the bowl.

4 Cover the apples with this topping mixture and then sprinkle the rest of the soft brown sugar over the top.

5 Put the pudding in the oven – remember to use oven gloves!

6 Bake the pudding for one hour. Turn off the oven.

7 Use the oven gloves to take the hot dish out of the oven.

8 Serve hot in bowls with cream or ice-cream – lovely! Some people had spoons made of horn with a silver whistle on the handle which they blew to ask for a second helping. I'm sure you will enjoy Morayshire Apples so much you will want a second helping too! You won't need a whistle!

Inter

Serves 4–6

1 hr 20 mins

Finish the dish with cream or ice-cream

Cook ≋

Oven ☐

Freeze ❋

Dunfillan Blackberry Pudding

Traditionally this pudding was made with brambles or blae-berries, but it can be made with any fruit you choose.

HAVE READY

110g (4oz) flour

50g (2oz) butter or margarine

50g (2oz) caster sugar

2 eggs

2 tablespoons milk

grated rind of 1 lemon

1 teaspoon baking powder

pinch of salt

saucepan

2-pint pie dish

2 mixing bowls

bowl scraper

knife + fork

teacup

sieve

wooden spoon

tablespoon

teaspoon

FILLING

450g (1lb) brambles or 1 tin prepared fruit

110g (4oz) sugar

TO MAKE

1 Arrange the shelves in the oven so that the pie dish can sit in the middle shelf of the oven. Heat the oven at Gas 4, 350°F or 180°C.

2 Put the fruit and sugar in the pan and set on the heat. Cook until the fruit is soft and juicy and the sugar has dissolved. This takes about 5 minutes. Turn off the heat.

3 Carefully spoon the fruit into the pie dish.

4 Break the eggs into the cup and mix them with the fork.

5 Put the sieve over a bowl, measure in the flour, baking powder and salt. Press through the sieve with the back of the tablespoon.

6 Put the butter and sugar in the other mixing bowl and mix them hard with the wooden spoon until you get a white and fluffy mixture – this is called 'beating' and it helps to get air into the mixture to make the sponge lighter.

7 Add the egg from the cup and a tablespoon of the flour mixture. Beat in with the wooden spoon.

8 Add the lemon rind, the rest of the flour mixture and the milk and stir gently together. That's the sponge made.

9 Scrape the sponge mixture into the pie dish with the bowl scraper. Smooth the sponge over the fruit with the back of the scraper.

10 Use the oven gloves to put the pie dish on the middle shelf in the oven. Bake the pudding for 20 minutes until it is risen and golden.

11 Carefully take the dish out of the oven using the oven gloves.

12 It is best to eat Dunfillan Blackberry Pudding while it is hot. And it tastes yummy on its own or with cream or custard. Try lifting the sponge with a spoon and putting ice-cream on top of the fruit inside. Marvellous!!!

Crannachan

This is also called 'Cream Crowdie' or 'Stapag' in the Highlands and 'Pram' in Shetland. It is a very old dish, traditionally made with whisky, and was usually eaten at festive occasions by the farming people. At harvest time or Hallowe'en lucky charms were mixed through the Crannachan — you can imagine that folk ate as much as they could in the hope of finding one!

Simple

Needs overnight soaking

Serves 4

30 mins

No Cook ☒

HAVE READY

110g (4oz) fresh raspberries (you can use strawberries, or a mixture of both)

50g (2oz) medium oatmeal

50g (2oz) cream cheese

2 tablespoons fruit juice

2 tablespoons honey (heather honey is best)

275 ml (½ pint) double cream

2 bowls

plate

whisk

bowl scraper

wooden spoon

tablespoon

dessertspoon

4 dessert glasses

damp cloth

TO MAKE

Put the oatmeal, honey and fruit juice into a bowl. Cover the bowl with the plate and leave overnight.

1. The next day, put the raspberries (all except 4 — keep these to decorate the top of each dessert) and the cream cheese into the bowl with the oatmeal, honey and fruit juice and mix everything together with the wooden spoon.

2. Set the other bowl on the damp cloth and pour in the double cream. Using the whisk — slowly at first so you do not splash — whip the cream until it stands up like mountain peaks. Stop beating or the cream will turn into butter. Tap the whisk on the side of the bowl to remove the cream.

3. Put a dessertspoon of cream into the bottom of each glass.

4. Divide the raspberry mixture between the four glasses. Use the bowl scraper to make sure you get all the mixture out of the bowl. Wash and dry the scraper.

5. Divide the remaining cream into the glasses and again use the scraper to get all the cream out of the bowl.

6. Place a raspberry on top of the Crannachan and put the glasses in the fridge to chill until it is time for you to eat.

Carageen Mould

Carageen is a brownish purple seaweed found on the coasts of North America and Europe. It is gathered from rock pools at the seashore, washed to remove the salt and sand, spread out on the rocks or on a white cloth on the grass and left to dry for several days. Carageen may be bought in health food shops or in the chemist. It is very good for you because it contains iron and sulphur, two elements which we need to keep healthy. Carageen is still used in Scotland and Ireland as an ingredient in food, particularly in puddings and drinks.

HAVE READY

12g (½oz) dried carageen

570ml (1 pint) milk

25g (1oz) sugar

1 cinnamon stick or lemon peel or a few drops vanilla essence for flavour

saucepan

bowl

wooden spoon

sieve

TO MAKE

1 Wash the carageen in cold water and soak in fresh cold water in the bowl for 20 minutes.

2 Hold the sieve over the sink and pour the carageen and water into it to drain off the water. Shake the seaweed.

3 Put the seaweed in the pan. Add the milk, sugar, cinnamon stick, lemon peel or vanilla essence. Wash the bowl and sieve.

4 Put the pan on a medium heat. Use the wooden spoon to stir the seaweed mixture as it comes to the boil.

5 When the mixture is bubbling, turn down the heat until the milk is just moving in the pan. Leave it to cook for 15 minutes until the seaweed is soft and the milk is thick.

6 Take the pan off the heat. Put the sieve over the bowl and pour the hot milk and seaweed into the sieve. This will strain out the seaweed and leave the thick milk in the bowl.

7 If you have a nice jelly mould, you can pour the milk into it. Leave it in a cool place to set.

8 Serve with fresh cream or ice-cream – it makes a lovely change from ordinary fruit jelly! What about adding milkshake syrup for a different flavour?

Simple

Needs to set

Serves 4

1 hr

Finish the dish with ice-cream

Cook ∭

Hob ◎

E. Wok ○

E. Fry ❖

105

Strawberry Sweet

This recipe comes from Aberdeenshire in the North East of Scotland. This special pudding is lovely with cool cream or ice-cream. The taste always makes me think of summer time.

Needs left
overnight

Serves 4

1 hr 45 mins

Cook ≋

Hob ◎

E. Wok ○

E. Fry ❖

HAVE READY

450g (1lb) ripe
strawberries

450g (1lb) redcurrants

450g (1lb) caster
sugar

150ml (¼ pint) cream

2 saucepans

large flat dish

sieve

wooden spoon

tablespoon

4 individual glasses

TO MAKE

Lay the strawberries on the flat dish and sprinkle half the caster sugar (225g/8oz) over them. Shake the dish gently so that the strawberries are all covered in sugar. Leave overnight.

1 The next day, put the redcurrants into the pan and place it on a low heat. The heat will make the redcurrants burst and all the juices will come out of them. This takes about 5 to 10 minutes.

2 Turn off the heat. Place the sieve over the other pan and pour the redcurrants into the sieve. Press the berries in the sieve with the back of the wooden spoon to squeeze out every drop of juice. Take the sieve off the pan and throw the skins and seeds away.

3 Add the rest of the sugar (225g/8oz) to the juice in the pan.

4 Put the pan on the heat. Hold the handle of the pan with one hand and use the wooden spoon to stir the sugar until it is dissolved.

5 Boil the juice and add the strawberries and sugar. Gently stir them into the juice with the wooden spoon.

6 When the fruit begins to boil up, turn down the heat until it is just bubbling and cook for 15 minutes. Leave the wooden spoon in the pan and this will stop the pan from boiling over. Fruit juices and sugar boil over very easily – they make quite a mess and can give you a nasty burn so be very careful.

7 After 15 minutes, turn off the heat. Let the pan cool for 30 minutes and then carefully spoon the fruit into the individual glasses.

8 Leave the Strawberrry Sweet to cool. A special pudding to eat with thick, cool cream or ice-cream – a taste of summertime!

The Story of Calfie's Cheese

Calfie's Cheese was a special treat which was given to the children of farming families at calving time. It is a sweet curd made from the milk from the first milking of the mother cow after the birth of the calf. This milk was strained and left in a warm place overnight. In the morning the milk had set like a soft cheese. The children ate the cheese sprinkled with sugar and thought it was wonderful.

Apple Frushie

This is a kind of fruit tart which is made in the west of Scotland. It was called Frushie because the pastry is crumbly and 'frushie' is an old Scottish word meaning 'crumbly'.

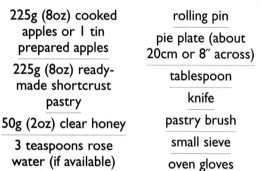

Inter

Serves 4

1 hr

Cook ♒

Oven ☐

Freeze ✳

HAVE READY

225g (8oz) cooked apples or 1 tin prepared apples

225g (8oz) ready-made shortcrust pastry

50g (2oz) clear honey

3 teaspoons rose water (if available)

rolling pin

pie plate (about 20cm or 8″ across)

tablespoon

knife

pastry brush

small sieve

oven gloves

TO MAKE

1 Arrange the oven shelves so that the tart can sit on the middle one. Switch on the oven at Gas 6, 425°F or 220°C.

2 Stew the apples (see page 6). Leave to cool.

3 Wash and dry your hands well. Clean the work surface. Shake some flour on the work surface and on the rolling pin. Take the pastry and roll it out to the thickness of a china plate. Try to make it big enough to fit the pie plate.

4 Lift the pastry on to the pie plate and press it gently into the plate using your knuckles. To trim off the edges, hold the pie plate up on the flat palm of one hand. Take the knife in your other hand and cut with the blade vertically round the edge of the plate. Keep the scraps.

5 Squash the scraps into one ball of pastry. Roll out the pastry until it is the same width as the pie plate.

6 Cut this piece into strips about 0.5cm (¼ inch) wide with the knife. These are for the top of the tart.

7 Spread the cooled stewed apples over the pastry in the pie plate using the back of the tablespoon.

8 Sprinkle the apples with the rose water and then pour the honey evenly over the top.

9 Wet the pastry brush in cold water and brush round the edge of the tart.

10 Lay the pastry strips on top of the apples, first going one way across the dish and then across the strips to make a criss-cross or 'lattice' design. Press the ends of the strips down on the wet edge of the tart, this will keep them in place.

11 Use the oven gloves to place the tart in the oven. Bake for 25 minutes until golden brown.

12 Take the hot tart from the oven – remember to use the oven gloves.

13 You can sprinkle some caster sugar over the top – this makes it look even better to eat! This is easy to do: get a small sieve, put some caster sugar in the sieve and shake it over the top of the tart.

14 Apple Frushie tastes delicious hot or cold – you decide!

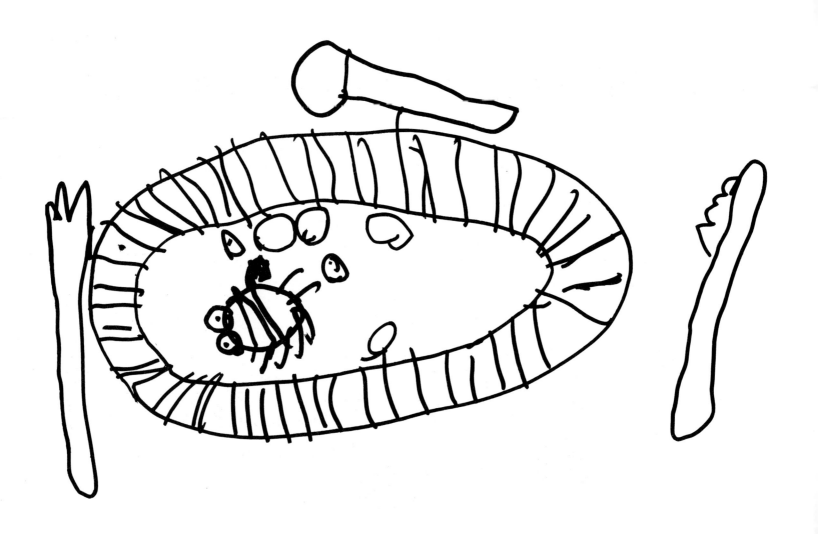

Snacks and Savouries

The Scots have always been proud of their kindness towards strangers; sometimes they have even argued among themselves as to who should give a meal and shelter to any visitor who came along! Even the poorest housewife would be pleased to welcome an extra person for a meal.

It was once the custom not to ask the name or business of a stranger until a year and a day had passed in case they were an enemy. The Scots took their care of strangers so seriously that they did not want to know if they had an enemy in their midst because they still would have felt obliged to give them hospitality!

Jolly Boys

Jolly Boys are made from an old Scottish favourite — black puddings. Black puddings were eaten as long ago as 1581 when Edinburgh Town Council moved the 'Puddin Mercat' to the 'Flesche Mercat' (meat market). They seem to have been popular with Scottish writers — Sir Walter Scott speaks of black puddings in his book *Old Mortality*, and James Hogg (the Ettrick Shepherd) wrote about a type of black pudding which was cooked in a frying pan.
They are still popular today and some fish and chip shops sell black pudding suppers — this is black pudding in batter served with chips.

HAVE READY

6 slices of black pudding (from the butcher or supermarket)

BATTER

3 tablespoons flour

I egg

milk

¼ teaspoon bicarbonate of soda

vegetable oil

I teaspoon salt

pinch pepper

deep-fat pan

mixing bowl

baking tray

flat plate

teacup

sharp knife

balloon whisk

draining spoon

kitchen towel

sieve

tablespoon

knife + fork

TO MAKE

1 Use the sharp knife to remove the skin from the black pudding. Lay the black pudding on the plate.

2 Place the sieve over the mixing bowl and pour in the flour. Push it through with the back of the spoon.

3 Add the bicarbonate of soda, salt and pepper.

4 Break the egg into the cup and pour it into the bowl with the flour.

5 Use the balloon whisk to stir the egg. While you are whisking add enough milk to make the mixture like very thick cream. (Add the milk a little at a time.) Whisk hard to take out all the lumps.

6 Put all the pieces of black pudding into the bowl and turn them in the batter so that they are all covered.

7 Jolly Boys are fried in deep oil which is very hot indeed so you must take extra care when cooking them. Heat the oil in the deep fat pan until it is the correct temperature – you can test the oil with a piece of dry bread. When the bread sizzles and turns brown the oil is ready.

8 Holding the bowl over the hot pan, take out each piece of battered pudding with the fork and *gently* drop them into the hot oil. (This will prevent drips of batter between the bowl and the pan.) Keep turning them with the draining spoon while they cook until both sides are golden brown. This takes a few minutes.

9 Put a layer of kitchen towel on the baking tray ready to drain the cooked Jolly Boys.

10 When the Jolly Boys are ready, lift them out of the fat on to the kitchen towel to drain off the extra oil.

11 Eat Jolly Boys with chips, baked beans, bacon, eggs, sausages – any way you like!

Cheese Pudding

The early Scottish housewife was very careful to use every scrap of food she had. Folk used to grow or catch all their food and could not afford to waste anything. There were no handy supermarkets! Cheese pudding is still a good way to use up stale bread, hard pieces of old cheese, extra milk and eggs.

Inter

Serves 2

45 mins

Cook ≋

Hob ◎

Oven ☐

HAVE READY

50g (2oz) breadcrumbs (4 slices of bread)

50g (2oz) cheese

275ml (½ pint) milk

12g (½oz) butter

2 eggs

½ teaspoon mustard powder (if available)

1 teaspoon salt

pinch pepper

saucepan

mixing bowl

2-pint pie dish

wooden spoon

small bowl

grater

knife + fork

teacup

teaspoon

oven gloves

TO MAKE

1 Arrange the shelves in the oven so that the pie dish will sit on the middle one. Heat the oven to Gas 4, 350°F or 180°C.

2 Grate the stale bread into crumbs in the mixing bowl. (If you have no stale bread, a frozen roll works very well). When you have enough breadcrumbs, grate the cheese into the crumbs in the bowl using the grooved side of the grater. Carefully remove crumbs or cheese sticking to the grater and take it out of the bowl.

3 Add mustard, salt and pepper.

4 Pour the milk into the pan. Add the butter and put the pan on the hob. Turn the heat to low and heat the milk so that the butter melts. Turn off the heat.

5 Break the egg into the cup and drop it into the small bowl. Do the same with the second egg. Mix them with the fork.

6 Tear off a piece of the paper from round the butter (or use a small piece of greaseproof paper with some butter on it) and rub the buttery side round the inside of the pie dish. This is called 'greasing', and it will stop the pudding from sticking to the dish.

7 Pour the eggs and warm milk into the bowl with the breadcrumbs and cheese and mix them all well together with the wooden spoon.

8 Pour the mixture into the pie dish and put it in the oven – remember to use oven gloves.

9 Bake the pudding for 30–40 minutes until it is risen and golden brown on top.

10 Use the oven gloves to take the dish from the oven. Check that the pudding is ready by pressing the top gently with your fingers – be careful as it will be very hot! It should be firm and spongy to touch when it is ready.

11 Eat cheese pudding immediately – you can eat it on its own or with crunchy raw carrots and other crisp raw vegetables.

Findon Toasts

Fast food was around long ago! This is a type of fast food which was eaten
hundreds of years before we heard of burgers! Finnan or Findon Haddock is named
after a fishing village near Aberdeen and is a kind of smoked haddock.
You could try kippers or other fish with this recipe – remember that Finnan Haddock
is already salty so you might have to add more salt when using a different fish.

Inter

Makes 4 slices
of toast

15 mins

Cook 〰

Hob ◎

E. Wok ◑

E. Fry ❖

116

HAVE READY

50g (2oz) cooked
Finnan Haddock (or
any smoked haddock)

4 slices of toast

25g (1oz) butter

1 tablespoon of cream

1 dessertspoon
chopped parsley

salt + pepper

saucepan

wooden spoon

plate

knife

TO MAKE

1 Put the butter in the saucepan and set it on the hob. Turn
   on the heat to low and melt the butter.

2 Add the fish and break it up with the wooden spoon. Add
   the cream and a pinch of salt and pepper. Stir well.

3 Heat the food through, stirring all the time. You will know
   when it is hot enough as it will begin to sizzle a little and
   steam. Turn off the heat when this happens.

4 Make the toast and spread one side with a little butter.
   Spread all 4 slices.

5 Divide the hot fish mixture between the four slices of toast
   and spread it over the toast with the knife.

6 Finally, sprinkle the chopped parsley on top – this is called
   a 'garnish'. Now your Findon Toasts are ready to eat. A
   quick snack with a difference!

Bacon Stacks

This recipe originated in the Lowlands where the land was more fertile and so grain could be grown. Therefore, the main difference in the diet of Scottish people was that the folk who lived in the Lowlands could make bread instead of the oatcakes which the Highlanders ate. They were also able to keep pigs and so they had plenty of bacon.

Simple

Serves 4

30 mins

Cook ♒

Oven ☐

HAVE READY

8 slices of bread

8 slices of cheese (175g/6oz or enough to cover the bread)

4 rashers of bacon

4 tomatoes

25g (1oz) butter

baking tray

sharp knife

chopping board

knife

fish slice

oven gloves

TO MAKE

1 Arrange the oven shelves so that the baking tray can sit on the middle one. Heat the oven at Gas 4, 350°F or 180°C.

2 Wash and dry the tomatoes. Carefully cut them into slices using the sharp knife.

3 Butter all 8 slices of bread on one side.

4 Lay a slice of cheese on each of the buttered slices.

5 Put some slices of tomato on top of the cheese.

6 Cut each rasher of bacon in two and place on top of the tomato slices.

7 Use the fish slice to put the Bacon Stacks on the baking tray and put the tray in the oven using the oven gloves. Bake for 20 minutes.

8 Take the tray from the oven with the oven gloves and use the fish slice to serve 2 slices on to each plate. Eat the Bacon Stacks while they are still hot. A tasty change from toasties!

117

Cheese Potato Cakes

This is a tasty way to use up left-over cooked potatoes – Cheese Potato Cakes are like fish cakes without the fish!

Adv

Serves 4

45 mins

Cook 〰

Hob ◎

E. Wok ○

E. Fry ❖

HAVE READY

225g (8oz) cold, cooked potatoes

110g (4oz) grated cheese

50g (2oz) flour

2 eggs

3 tablespoons butter

½ teaspoon salt

golden breadcrumbs

vegetable oil to fry

some milk

frying pan

saucepan

large mixing bowl

2 large flat plates

small bowl

potato masher

grater

teacup

knife

fish slice

tea towel

kitchen towel

wooden spoon

tablespoon

teaspoon

TO MAKE

1 Grate the cheese into the small bowl using the grooved side of the grater. Use your fingers to carefully remove any cheese sticking to the grater. Take the grater out of the bowl.

2 Break an egg into the teacup and drop it into the small bowl with the cheese. Do the same with the second egg.

3 Put the butter in the saucepan and set it on the hob. Turn on the heat to low and melt the butter. Turn off the heat, take the pan off the cooker and place it on a heat-resistant surface.

4 Put the potatoes in the mixing bowl and mash them with the potato masher. Pour in the melted butter.

5 Add the flour, salt, cheese and eggs. Mix them all together with the wooden spoon. If the mixture is too stiff, add one tablespoonful of milk at a time until the mixture is like the stiffness of play dough.

6 Wash the work surface and dry it with a clean tea towel. Shake a little flour over the top and then scrape the mixture from the mixing bowl on to the flour. Shake a little flour on top of the mixture.

7 Wash and dry your hands really well. Rub some flour on them to stop the cheese potato cakes from sticking to them.

8 Take a little of the mixture and shape it into a small flat cake about 5cm across and 1cm deep. Do this until you have used up all the mixture.

9 Clean all the flour off the work surface. (A quick way to do this is to scrape it all off with the blade of a palette knife. Pile the flour in a heap and then put it in the bin.) Wipe over with a clean damp cloth and dry with a tea towel.

10 Take a square of kitchen towel and shake a heap of golden crumbs in the middle. Take one of the cakes and put it in the crumbs. Lift up the corners of the towel and shake the crumbs over the top of the cake and then press down with the palm of your hand to make sure that the crumbs are stuck. Put the cake on to the plate. Do this with all the cakes.

11 Put the plate of coated cakes in the fridge to chill for 15 minutes. This makes them firmer and easier to cook.

12 Lay some kitchen towel on a plate to drain the oil from the cakes so they are not greasy. Set the plate beside the hob.

13 Put enough oil in the frying pan to cover the bottom and place it on the hob. Turn on the heat to medium. To test when the oil is ready, drop a piece of bread in the oil, if it sizzles and turns brown the oil is ready.

14 Fry the cakes in the hot oil, turning once with the fish slice, until they are golden on both sides. Place them on the kitchen towel.

15 You can eat hot Cheese Potato Cakes on their own or with anything you like – how about crispy raw vegetables, baked beans, sweetcorn, or even spaghetti shapes? Have you any ideas? Cheese Potato Cakes are also tasty cold as a snack or for a picnic – try them as something new in your lunch box at school.

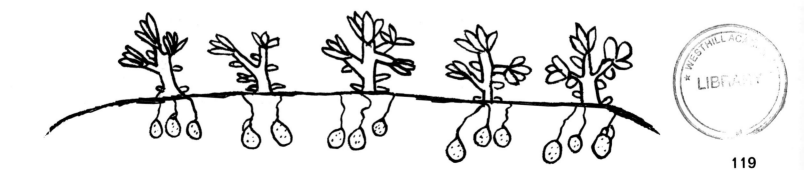

Boudinettes

I am not sure where this recipe comes from but the name sounds French. Perhaps you could eat them with French bread!

Adv

Serves 4

30 mins

Cook ≋

Hob ◎

E. Wok ○

E. Fry ❖

120

HAVE READY

225g (8oz) cold, cooked potatoes

110g (4oz) cold, cooked bacon

25g (1oz) butter

2 tablespoons milk

4 tablespoons flour

1 tablespoon chopped parsley

vegetable oil to fry

1 teaspoon salt

pinch pepper

frying pan

baking tray

mixing bowl

large plate

rolling pin

large scone cutter

kitchen towel

fish slice

potato masher

chopping board

sharp knife

fork

tablespoon

teaspoon

TO MAKE

1 Put the cooked bacon on to the chopping board and cut into very small pieces with the sharp knife.

2 Put the potatoes into the mixing bowl and mash them with the potato masher.

3 Add the butter, milk, flour, salt and pepper. Mash them all together with the potato masher until you have a smooth mixture.

4 Wash and dry the work surface. Shake some flour over the surface and on to the rolling pin. Turn the potato mixture out of the bowl on to the flour and shake some more flour over the top

5 Roll out the mixture until it is about the thickness of a china plate. Use the scone cutter to cut it into large circles.

6 Lay 1 teaspoon chopped bacon at the edge of the circle and then roll it up.

7 Press the edges together with your fingers.

8 Lay them on the plate and put it beside the hob.

9 Pour oil into the frying pan to cover the bottom. Put the pan on the hob and turn on the heat. (The oil is hot enough when a piece of bread dropped in the oil turns golden brown.)

10 Use the fish slice to place the Boudinettes in the oil and fry. Hold the handle of the frying pan and use the fish slice and fork to turn them after a couple of minutes. Fry until golden on both sides – this takes 4 to 5 minutes.

11 Place a layer of kitchen towel on the baking tray. Set it beside the hob

12 Place the Boudinettes on to the kitchen towel with the fish slice to drain off the oil.

13 Your Boudinettes are ready as a hot snack – they are much better than pies or sausage rolls and will make a great surprise for your friends.

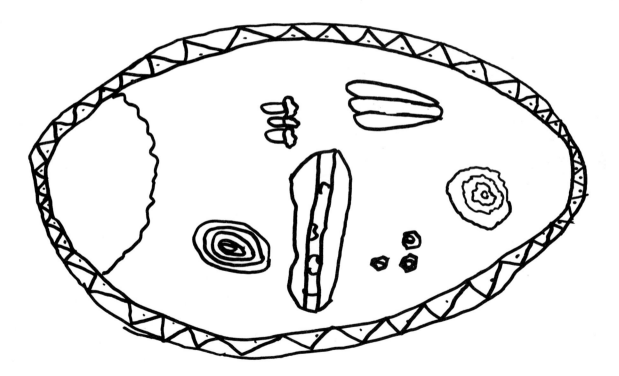

Farm Cheese Patties

The country families of Scotland used to live in small cottages called a 'but 'n' ben'. The 'but' was the kitchen where the family ate and lived. There was a shelf for all the crockery and dishes, a chair for the man and small stools called 'creepies' for the woman and children. The cooking was done on the hearth of the open fire, or sometimes over the fire on a metal frame which held the pots and pans.

HAVE READY

220g (8oz) grated cheese

220g (8oz) shortcrust pastry

4 eggs

4 teacupfuls of milk

flour to roll out the pastry

vegetable oil

pinch of nutmeg

pinch of cayenne pepper

salt + pepper

tray of bun tins

mixing bowl

pastry brush

tablespoon

teaspoon

2 teacups

knife + fork

grater

rolling pin

large scone cutter

oven gloves

TO MAKE

1 Arrange the shelves in the oven so that there is a shelf in the middle for the tray of patty tins. Heat the oven at Gas 6, 400°F or 200°C.

2 Wash and dry the work surface. Shake a little flour over the worktop and lay the pastry on the flour. Shake some flour on the top of the pastry and then over the rolling pin.

3 Roll out the pastry to the thickness of a china plate. Cut out 12 circles (these are called 'rounds') with the scone cutter.

4 Collect all the scraps of pastry and press them together with your hands. Roll the pastry out again and cut out another 12 rounds with the scone cutter.

5 Pour a little vegetable oil into the teacup. Dip the pastry brush in the oil and run it round the inside of 12 bun tins – this will stop the pastry from sticking.

6 Wash and dry the brush and teacup.

7 Gently lift a round of pastry and put it in a patty tin. Press it in using your knuckles.

8 Grate the cheese into the bowl using the grooved side of the grater. Use your fingers to carefully remove any cheese sticking to the grater. Take the grater out of the bowl.

9 Break an egg into the teacup and pour it into the mixing bowl. Do this with the other egg.

10 Add the milk, nutmeg, cayenne (a pinch is the amount of spice you can hold between your thumb and finger) half a teaspoon of salt and some pepper. Use the fork to mix it all together.

11 Use the tablespoon to spoon the mixture from the mixing bowl into each pastry case. Place a round of pastry over the top of each patty tin and then gently press down round the edges with your fingers.

12 Pour a little milk into the teacup, then brush some milk over the top of the small pies with the pastry brush.

13 Use the oven gloves to put the tray into the hot oven. Bake the pies for 10 minutes then turn down the heat to Gas 4, 350°F or 180°C for another 10 minutes.

14 Farm Cheese Patties are really good hot with a crispy salad, and you can eat them cold too – make them the next time you plan to go on a picnic.

Make your own personal Farm Cheese Patties by adding chopped onion; chopped tomato; chopped chives; chopped apple; chopped, cooked broccoli; chopped, cooked bacon or cold chopped ham. Remember to reduce the amount of cheese to 175g (6oz) when adding other ingredients.

Toasted Cheese

This recipe for Toasted Cheese was a great favourite of Lord Lauderdale of Thirlestane Castle. In his recipe he says that the cheese should be roasted but not boiled.

Inter

Serves 2

20 mins

Finish the dish
with toast

Cook ≋

Hob ◎

E. Wok ○

E. Fry ❖

Grill ⌘

HAVE READY

110g (4oz) cheese –
Dunlop or single
Gloucester are best

50g (2oz) butter

1 egg

1 tablespoon cream

saucepan

oven-proof dish
(½ pint to 1 pint)

plate

teacup

knife

tablespoon

TO MAKE

1 Put the cheese on the plate and cut it into slices.

2 Tip the cheese into the pan, add the cream and butter and put the pan on a low heat.

3 Stir the mixture with the wooden spoon until it all melts together and boils. It will start to bubble and become smooth.

4 Turn off the heat and set the pan on a heat-resistant surface.

5 Break the egg into the cup and slowly pour it into the pan, stirring all the time with the wooden spoon. Stir until all the egg has disappeared into the mixture.

6 Remove the grill pan and turn on the grill to high.

7 Pour the cheese mixture out of the saucepan into the oven proof dish. Put the oven proof dish under the grill (use the oven gloves). Cook for 4 to 5 minutes, watching all the time until the top is golden brown.

8 Turn off the grill and use oven gloves to lift the hot dish out from under the grill.

9 The toasted cheese is best eaten hot with freshly toasted bread.

The Baxter Story

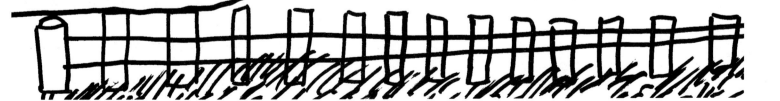

The Baxter family business was born 128 years ago in a little grocery shop on Spey Street, Fochabers – George Baxter's. The grocer's wife, Margaret, made some strawberry jam in the back shop. It was good jam. George asked her to make more for him to sell in his front shop. Margaret's jams became very popular with the villagers, the local gentry and the ladies from many of the villages around Speyside.

In due course, George's eldest son, William, joined the business and opened the village store's wholesale department. On his bicycle, armed with his samples, he went to offer jams made to his mother's delicious recipes, to other shops in distant corners of the country. Later, tea, coffee and many other grocery products were added to Willie Baxter's sales list.

In 1914, William and his wife, Ethel, who was also a very keen cook, decided to build a new factory across the river from Fochabers with local stone, and the roof timbers came from a cargo ship which had been washed ashore on a local beach. The fertile soils of Moray provided the small factory with marvellous fruit and vegetables, and from the surrounding hills and glens came the freshest of game. In 1929, Ethel produced Royal Game Soup, which was to become known all over the world and today is one of the world's best-selling quality soups. This was the beginning of Baxter's current family of fine foods.

The next generation, Gordon and Ian, continued in their parent's footsteps by working together to make the Baxter business the success story it is today. After the last war, Gordon and Ian returned to a business employing only 11 people of the original 35. It was very hard work, but they were determined to build the business and to base it on quality products, using traditional, wholesome ingredients, such as could be found in their mother's Royal Game Soup. Gordon's wife, Ena, too, has played a major role in the development of Baxters of Speyside, creating new recipes and cooking on television.

Today, Gordon and Ena's children, the fourth generation, are actively involved in the running of this still very independent, family-owned company. Audrey, Andrew and Michael continue in the commitment and dedication to being the best in the field and to seeing their own children become part of the wider Baxter story.

Bibliography

Recommended reading for more adventurous recipes and for further information on Scottish traditional cooking

Brown, Catherine, *Scottish Regional Recipes* (Penguin)
Brown, Catherine, *Broths to Bannocks* (John Murray)
Fitzgibbon, Theodora, *Traditional Scottish Cookery* (Fontana)
Fitzgibbon, Theodora, *A Taste of Scotland* (Pan)
The Glasgow Cookery Book (John Smith)
Kirk, E. W., *Tried Favourites Cookery Book* (A. D. Johnston Edinburgh,
      Horace Marshall & Son, London)
MacLaren, Kate, M., *Mrs MacLaren's Cookery Book* (Moray & Nairn
      Newspaper Co.)
McNeill, Marian, F., *The Scots Kitchen* (Blackie & Son)
McNeill, Marian, F., *The Scots Cellar* (Lochar Publishing)
The Scottish Women's Rural Institute Cookery Book (sixth edition) (S.W.R.I.
      Edinburgh)

Index